WONDERS OF A TREASURE TROVE TO ALLAH

Regina Woods

Copyright © 2024

All Rights Reserved

ISBN:

Disclaimer

I am a woman, a Muslim, a wife, a mother, a mother-in-law, a grandmother, an aunt, a great aunt, a sister, a niece, a cousin, a real estate referral agent, a retiree, a neighbor, a citizen, and a confidant. I am not a lawyer, doctor, counselor, scientist, scholar, therapist, psychiatrist, police officer, or judge. I talk about my experiences and the experiences of people who have confided in me and those that I have observed through friendship, social events, private affairs, and frenemies (people who pretend to be your friends). I live my life for the worship of Allah (swt), and prayer and the Qur'an are my food for thought and my soul. I believe that there is so much wisdom in the Qur'an, and based on my experiences and others, I relate to the Qur'an, and I hope, from my view, I have imparted what I feel is the heart of the Qur'an.

Dedication

This book is dedicated to Allah Ta'ala for all the favors He has bestowed upon me. He allowed me to grow with my twin brother in my mother's womb. He called me to Islam and allowed me to do Hajj with ease. He comforts me through all my trials and tribulations and joys. I ask Allah the Glorious, the Most High to accept my worship and forgive any mistake I have made. Allah Ta'ala says remember me in a gathering, and I will remember you in a bigger and better gathering.

Acknowledgment

I thank my ancestors for I truly feel someone prayed for me a long, long time ago. I thank my grandparents because of the stability and foundation they instilled in my life. I thank my mother because she did her best to raise eleven children. I thank my father, whom I barely knew because he died early in my life, which made me ponder and wonder about him and life a lot. I thank my stepdad for being around. I thank all those neighbors and friends and those who aided in my safety and showed me mercy and love as I ran the streets as a wild child. I thank my ten brothers and sisters for giving me experiences to talk about. I thank my special cousin-in-law, who took me under her wing and taught me to be conscious of God. I thank my husband for being my husband because he, too, made me ponder and wonder. I thank my children whom Allah (swt) gifted to me. It was and is because of them that I wanted to pray and change my way. I want to be an example. I thank my grandchildren as they made me believe Allah (swt) is true because, at one time, I thought I would never live to be old. Most importantly, I thank Allah (swt) for compelling me toward the deen of Islam.

Table of Contents

Disclaimer 3
Dedication iv
Acknowledgment v
About the Author ix
Summary 1
My Epitome 1 5
    Allah's Gift 7
    Beauty 9
    Pleasing You 11
    The Sweetness of Joy 12
    I Love You 14
    Is it Possible? 16
    Why is the Question 18
    The Era of Time 20
My Epitome 2 22
    This Struggle Is Real 24
    This World 26
    Forgive Me 28
    Limited Understanding 31
    How Do You Know 33
    My Heart 35
    I Still Weep 37
    It's Okay 39
    Why Me 41
    It's Me 43
    The Rope 45
    No Reason 47

My Epitome 3 49
- Open Enemy 51
- The Veil 53
- Coward 55
- You Thief 59
- Don't Worry 61
- Woe 63
- Beyond Bounds 65
- Three Meals and a Pot 67
- Sins of the Heart 69
- Don't Get Angry 71
- Death 73

My Epitome 4 75
- My Lifeline 77
- Habibah 78
- Momma Knows 80
- She Calls Herself Niya 82
- From the Womb 84
- Sister 86
- It Hurts 88
- WHY? 90
- Muslims 92

My Epitome 5 94
- When You Know 96
- My Soul 98
- I Want It 100
- It's Funny 102
- I Believe 104

My Epitome 6 106
    My Love 110
    Open to Me 111
    Woman 113
    If Loving You 114
    To You I Tweet 116
    Do You Really Listen 118
    A Vicious Cycle 120
    Happiness 122
Epitome 7 124
    Food 128
    Jump 130
    Talk About It 132
    The Will 133
    Merciful 135
    Spreading the Love 136
    I'm Stuck Like That 138
Index 141

About the Author

Regina Woods is a Muslim woman who has dedicated her life to learning and spreading her religion.

Regina and her twin brother, Reginald, were born in an era when neighbors cared. They were able to go outside and play until the street lights came on. It was because of the love of family, friends, neighbors, and, of course, the grace of Allah (swt) that she is alive today. It truly takes a village to raise a child.

She is thankful for everything she has experienced in this life and how Allah (swt) has helped her throughout it all. Regina believes we can worship in all that we do by not being idle. When she is not writing or helping others, she sews as a hobby and plays scrabble for fun.

Page Blank Intentionally

Summary

We all have trials and tribulations, and although Allah (swt) won't allow us to suffer more than we can bear, somehow, the trials seem very heavy. For me, I found comfort in keeping a diary of my daily struggles and blessings. I tried recording my blessings as a reminder to be thankful for what I had, but as the Qur'an states, we can't count all the favors of Allah (swt). My list of blessings was so long that when you count the many car accidents Allah (swt) blocked, the many head bumps among my children, grandchildren, and myself Allah (swt) healed, the many fights and arguments Allah (swt) averted from me, they can't be counted. However, knowing all that, I became bored with writing my daily diary because it seemed my daily life was such a struggle. So, I stopped writing.

Some time passed before I could write again. However, I believe Allah (swt) inspired me through consciousness and soul searching to write poetry as opposed to keeping a diary. Something I could cling to as a motto for life. Pain and confusion seemed to be my biggest test, and talking to people about my innermost vulnerabilities that I could not trust. In the past, it was drugs and alcohol I sought to cope. However, I begged Allah (swt) to change my condition. Once I came to Allah (swt) with a sincere heart and action to implement that changed heart, Allah (swt) allowed my heart to rest. So, pain and confusion are still there, but my method of coping is Allah (swt).

Doctors will prescribe psychiatry or medicine or drugs, which, in some cases, may be necessary. However, I believe we should seek Allah (swt), the Master Counselor, first. Just like to lose weight and be healthy, some of us opt to diet and exercise; the problem is that some of us don't sincerely do what we have to do to achieve that goal. Likewise, we really haven't sincerely given Allah (swt) our hearts. For me, however, life had taken such a toll. I was tired and worn down by the highs and lows of life. I submitted and committed to seeking Allah (swt). Since I found Islam, by the grace of Allah (swt), my heart has been at rest. Pain and suffering are still there, but Allah (swt) allows me to cope by doing what is pleasing to Him. An idle heart and hands will lead you to trouble. As stewardesses of the earth, we know our purpose, which is to worship Allah (swt), but we must find our calling.

When I first entered college, I wanted to be a nurse, but my academic scores were not enough. So, I changed my major. As I got older, I thought I wanted to care for the elderly or young, but Allah (swt) allowed me to experience some things, and I realized it was not for me. I used to think I wanted to start an after-school program for children in need of mentoring, but my finances were not sufficient. We plan, but Allah (swt) is the best of planners. In 1990, by the grace and mercy of Allah (swt), I saw the need to support my brother. He had been in jail already for eight years since 1982, and I was supporting him, but not the way I wanted to. I vowed to Allah (swt) to support my brother, Carmen, with all my heart, and I have been supporting him ever since then. He is incarcerated for a murder he did not commit, and my prayer is for Allah (swt) to free him from his incarceration. Allah (swt), in His beneficent wisdom, used my brother to introduce me to Islam. Prior to Islam, for most of my life, I wondered where I fit. However, when I submitted and committed myself to Allah (swt), I stopped wondering and started doing.

Reading the Qur'an is truly a comfort for me. Happy, sad, angry, or confused, when I read the Qur'an, it soothes me. I believe it makes me feel closer to Allah (swt). I love Allah (swt) unseen. Yet, Shaytan bombards me with whispers questioning my love for Allah (swt) unseen. I believe when I fell out the window as a child, I had a near-death experience. Whether it was a dream or my soul was actually there, I was in the most angelic place made of gold and glass, and the acoustics were so clear. My voice when I spoke sounded like music. What I'm trying to say is that this vision has been with me all my life. I want to go back there.

Moreover, by the grace and mercy of Allah (swt), I gave birth to two beautiful children who developed in my womb from a clot of blood into a body with unique fingers, toes, hair, etc. I witnessed that. The grass grows, dies, and grows back again and again. A prelude to the resurrection, yet man can only plant the seed. Allah (swt) is the designer of its matter. I cannot see Allah (swt), but Allah (swt) has allowed me to see His creation. The sun and moon are in their orbits, the wind's fury, yet ships sail the seas because of it. There is so much in creation to see Allah (swt). So yes, I love Allah (swt), and His word comforts me. It is food for my soul.

We all have souls, and when the body is dead, the soul will live on. The whereabouts of the souls are something that only Allah (swt) knows! When I write poetry about Allah's word, it holds me. If I am feeling sad, angry, joyous, hurt, etc., I cling to the poems that I wrote as a motto of life to comfort and inspire me. My twin brother was part of a fraternity, and he learned a motto – "EXCUSES" – which he also taught to me. It stuck with me in my heart. Excuses are tools of incompetence; those who excel in them seldom excel in anything else. It became a way of life for me, a motivator when I didn't want to, and enlightenment when I achieved so much power in those words. Words are powerful, and Allah's word is angelic, mesmerizing, soothing, healing, awakening, and more. I love Allah (swt), and I love humanity. The trials are heavy, that is for sure, but Paradise without Hell would have never been cherished. I write to soothe my soul and spread Allah's word in the hope of Paradise for myself and mankind.

My Epitome 1

Allah's gift is the Qur'an, which explains the beauty of creation and its signs. Life is trying, and we all suffer trying times, so sometimes we forget to see the beauty of life. Allah (swt) created us for a reason, and that is to be tested – the test of worshiping Allah (swt), our Creator. I ponder about life a lot because it seems the world is so cruel, but if we had light without darkness, we would never know the beauty of the light. There is beauty in Allah's creation: the southern lights, the rainbow, the coral reef, the sunset, the sunrise, the changing seasons, the stars, etc. It is easy to feel pain because pain hurts; therefore, it is long-lasting. However, joy is rewarding yet short-lived in most cases; short-lived because we easily forget. This is why Allah (swt) tells us in the Qur'an to ponder about His creation. There is beauty in creation, which fills your heart with love for the Creator, the creatures, and one another. This is why we flock to the beaches to soak up the sun and feel its warmth, which soothes the soul, if only for a while. It is imperative to admire the beauty of the creation and the love of the Creator.

The sun's job is to give us energy, light, warmth, and comfort, and it does its job well. So, Allah's creation not only beautifies the heavens and the earth, but it is multi-purpose. Yet, some like it hot, and some like it cold, for there is nothing like the fresh, clean air of snow-covered mountains and forest, which, too, is good for the soul and body. There is beauty and love in Allah's creation. Love is in the air flowing from you to me, giving us the joy and satisfaction of knowing and observing the signs of Allah's creation.

Bism Allah Al-Rahman Al-Rahim

Allah's Gift

Allah's gift is the Qur'an; **read it** and believe it. It is enriched with signs.

Evolution was Darwin's theory. If you want to **know the truth** about the creation, **read Qur'anic stories.**

The **Big Bang,** that is what scientists call it. Allah (swt) said **"Be" and it was**. Then, **matter** expanded.

Dust particles, gases that took billions of years to form nebulae, stars, planets, black holes, and white dwarfs are some things that scientists found bizarre.

Prophet Muhammad (saw) revealed these phenomena in about 700 AD. The **sun** and **moon** running their course. **Qur'an Surah 10 Yūnus Ayats 4-7** is absolutely the **original source.**

Isaac Newton's law of mutual attraction of bodies was considered to be a greater discovery. However, what he discovered came **hundreds** of years later.

Signs of creation are found **throughout the Qur'an.** The three layers of the ocean's depth, fingerprinting, the forelock, the stages of conception, and much more are why scientists go to **deep space to explore.**

Exploring the cosmos, looking for earth-like planets, **seven heavens, and of the earth the like, that is Qur'anic.**

Allah's gift is the Qur'an. Read it and believe it. It is enriched with signs. The worlds exist not by a flute but **by Allah's design.**

Recommended Reading:

- Surah 36 Yā-Sin Ayats 33-40
- Surah 23 Al-Mu'minūn Ayats 12-22*
- Surah 10 Yūnus Ayats 3-9
- Surah 21 Al-Anbiyā' Ayats 30-40
- Surah 81 At-Takwir Ayats 1-29**
- Surah 41 Ha mim Al Sajdah Ayats 9-12*
- Surah 79 An-Nāzi'āt Ayats 27-33
- Surah 67 Al-Mulk Ayats 1-30*
- Surah 55 Ar-Rahmān Ayats 1-43**
- Surah 30 Ar-Rūm Ayats 43-53

Bism Allah Al-Rahman Al-Rahim

Beauty

Beauty is everywhere. Allah (swt) created beauty for all to share.

The trees with all their beautiful colors, the moon that lights the night, the sun that gives us warmth, the stars that shine so bright, the wind that cools the heat, the birds that sing Allah's glory, the clouds that spray its mist, the rainbow that has a story, the bees that give us honey, and the monkey whose play is so funny.

Beauty is everywhere. Allah (swt) created beauty for all to share.

The baby in the cradle, the brokenhearted mended, the orphan fed, the poor no more, the wayward found, the righteous crowned, the slave released – **WOW!** That feels like peace.

Beauty is everywhere. Allah (swt) created beauty for all to share.

Recommended Reading:

- Surah 10 Yūnus Ayats 5-6
- Surah 23 Al-Mu'minūn Ayats 10-22

- Surah 21 Al-Anbiyā' Ayats 30-33
- Surah 36 Yā-Sin Ayats 33-40
- Surah 53 An-Najm Ayats 40-48
- Surah 55 Ar-Rahmān Ayats 1-25
- Surah 76 Ad-Dahr Ayats 7-12

Wonders of a Treasure Trove to Allah

Bism Allah Al-Rahman Al-Rahim

Pleasing You

I am happy Allah (swt) because of the joy and satisfaction. You allowed me to put our plan into action.

To think, pleasing you in my works, I am truly the one who benefits from the perks, **not** money, fame, or status, **but the perks** of **love, charity,** and **the real stuff** that matters.

This feeling might **only last a moment,** but somehow, I feel I'll remember it until atonement.

I am happy, Lord, because of the **joy and satisfaction.** This work for you, I have **gained** such a passion.

Pleasing you is pleasing me. **This feeling,** I want for **ALL** humanity.

Recommended Reading:

- Surah 53 An-Najm Ayats 39-48
- Surah 76 Ad-Dahr or Al-Insan Ayats 5-26
- Surah 32 Al-Sajdah Ayats 16-19
- Surah 25 Al-Furqān Ayats 63-76

Bism Allah Al-Rahman Al-Rahim

The Sweetness of Joy

Reading the Qur'an and hearing **your words testifying to me,** Allah (swt), is the sweetness of joy.

I delight in truth. The stars and galaxies bursting in the universe – creation at its best – is proof.

The earth was dark, but then you gave us light. The sun, its heat, its warmth that radiates so bright.

The depth of the mountains keeps the earth from **shaking**. The planets moving in their orbits are all due to your making.

I delight in truth. The conception and deliverance of my babies are proof.

The sweetness of joy, **the salvation of my progeny, would be the greatest reward.**

Our souls soar and explore as we sleep. That is **the** ultimate reflection of what we seek.

I delight in truth. The pillars holding back the universe from falling to earth. I don't think mankind understands **Allah's value** of our worth.

Protection has been granted if we make the choice. The heavenly hosts are watching, recording, and listening to our voice.

I delight in truth, truth, for your words testify to me. Your signs are clear for those you have bestowed knowledge to see.

The sweetness of joy is you, Allah (swt). You encompass my past, present, and future, and I submit to you, your humble servant and obedient creature with all my flaws.

Recommended Reading:

- Surah 32 Al-Sajdah Ayats 16-19
- Surah 39 Az-Zumar Ayats 33-42**
- Surah 36 Yā-Sin Ayats 33-40
- Surah 25 Al-Furqān Ayats 47-59
- Surah 21 Al-An'biyā Ayats 30-33

Regina Woods

Bism Allah Al-Rahman Al-Rahim

I Love You

I love you, **Allah (swt),** for so many reasons. **You allowed me not to be a heathen.**

You comfort my heart **with your word.**

You allow **me to speak** and be heard.

You protect me **from me.**

Your signs you allow me to see.

You constantly **keep** Shaytan at bay.

You allow me **in your name** to pray.

You **forgive me** for **my weakness.**

You **instilled** in me **a uniqueness.**

You **bless me** with **your grace.**

You gave me a **home** and **place.**

You wake me **seeking you every day.**

You **keep me** from going astray.

You inspire me to forbid evil and do good.

You have **given me** health, wealth, and knowledge I have understood.

Most importantly, I love you because I believe your promise to be true. **Paradise is the home of the believer.** I hope to be one of its receivers. **Even more,** I love you through **all my foretold trials:** the car incidents, the brutal attacks, and falling out of the window as a child. I really feel you have my back. **You saved me from ALL Shaytan's attacks.** I love you, Allah (swt), for all that and more, but if we were keeping score, **I know you love me more.**

Recommended Reading:

- Surah 53 An-Najm Ayats 39-48
- Surah 76 Ad-Dahr or Al-Insan Ayats 5-26
- Surah 29 Al'Ankabūt Ayats 42-44
- Surah 30 Ar-Rūm Ayats 17-31
- Surah 32 Al-Sajdah Ayats 16-19
- Surah 34 Al-Saba' Ayat 6

Bism Allah Al-Rahman Al-Rahim

Is it Possible?

Is it possible that life exists in other worlds? The universe is always in a constant twirl.

Twirling, moving, spinning according to Allah's laws, **all matter** must answer our Master's call.

The Qur'an mentions **seven heavens and of the earth the like.** If life doesn't exist in other worlds, **then why mention seven?**

Jinns and angels we don't see, but as we can only feel the wind's presence and never capture a glean, **Allah (swt) chose the angels and jinns** to be of the **world of the unseen.** Yet, on earth, we all coexist.

Coexist as the planets in the galaxies twirl. So, is it possible for life to exist in other worlds?

We don't know **what we don't know.** Discovery is a challenge, and deep space is where humans choose to go.

Allah (swt) is the **One** and **Only** who can unlock the mysteries of the unknown, but Allah (swt) gave us **the Qur'an** and other signs that lead to **His throne.**

Wonders of a Treasure Trove to Allah

Recommended Reading:

- Surah 6 Al-An'ām Ayat 59
- Surah 65 At-Talāq Ayat 12-13**
- Surah 55 Ar-Rahmān 31-33**
- Surah 25 Al-Furqān Ayats 56-77*
- Surah 17 Al-Isrā Ayat 70*
- Surah 30 Ar-Rūm Ayats 8-30*
- Surah 35 Fātir Ayats 9-18 & 38-45*
- Surah 37 As-Saffāt Ayats 11-44*
- Surah 81 At-Takwir Ayats 26-29*

Bism Allah Al-Rahman Al-Rahim

Why is the Question

Why waiver about mankind being part of a multiverse or in a simulation? **The Qur'an tells us that Allah (swt) has created worlds, that everything has been measured, and that we are being observed.** Stop playing, read, and learn Allah's word!

The heavenly host are watching and recording, too, all of what mankind do.

You claim mankind evolved from apes. Homo Erectus came down out of the tree, built fires, walked on two legs, and had tiny brain shapes.

Or, Lucy the Australopithecus afarensis, whose bones were discovered in Ethiopia. **All these communities of the genus Homo are scientists' utopias.**

Hominins are defined by their fossils, preferably their bone structure and social similarities to mankind. However, **their molecular DNA** makes them a different species, and that is based on Allah's design.

Scientists claim the two species interbred, but the **genus Homo** is extinct and **No Longer Exists.** So, again, what they speculate is conjecture with a twist.

Conjectures will always be guesses, hypotheses, theories, or speculations. However, chimpanzees, gorillas, or any kind of apes with their 48 chromosomes and mankind with our 46 chromosomes have **no fertile relations.**

Allah (swt) created mankind, and we are being observed. **Please, please, please read and learn Allah's word!**

Recommended Reading:

- Surah 50 Qāf Ayats 1-34**
- Surah 43 Az-Zukhruf Ayats 74-89*
- Surah 15 Al-Hijr Ayats 26-28
- Surah 36 Yā-Sin Ayats 33-40
- Surah 82 Al-Infitār Ayats 10-12
- Surah 35 Fātir Ayats 11-35*
- Surah 27 An-Naml Ayats 57-79**
- Surah 10 Yūnus Ayats 31-41 & 60-66
- Surah 76 Ad-Dahr Ayats 23-31
- Suraha 56 Al-Wāqi'ah Ayats 57-77*

Bism Allah Al-Rahman Al-Rahim

The Era of Time

The time of **Prophet Noah (as)** was the ark. The people didn't believe, so they became food for the sharks.

The time of **Prophet Ibraheem (as),** nations were born. Because of Allah's decree, families were torn.

The time of **Prophet Yusuf (as)** were interpretations of dreams. Allah (swt) established him in the King's kingdom to be supreme.

The time of **Prophet Musa (as)**, the scriptures were divine. Pharoah was forbidden to cross the ocean's line.

The time of **Prophet Easah (as)** was the miracle of all miracles, for the baby was born who spoke from the cradle.

The time of **Prophet Muhammad (saw),** the last and final Prophet, **is SIGNS,** foretold signs, signs that are blowing scientist's minds.

Scientists' calculations and studies are only now manifesting what has already been known. The **SIGNS** of **creation that lead to Allah's throne!**

Wonders of a Treasure Trove to Allah

Recommended Reading:

- Surah 25 Al-Furqān Ayats 56-77
- Surah 30 Ar-Rūm Ayats 8-35
- Surah 2 Al-Baqarah Ayats 83-101
- Surah 3 Al-Imran Ayats 45-67
- Surah 33 Al-Ahzāb Ayats 38-48*
- Surah 37 As-Saffāt Ayats 75-149*
- Surah 71 Nūh Ayats 21-28*
- Surah 12 Yūsuf Ayats 4-57

My Epitome 2

It is true that if we had light without darkness, we would not know the value of light. Likewise, if we have Paradise without Hell, Paradise would never be cherished. Life struggles are real. I was born with a twin in a large family. My mother was sick, and my father died early in my life. From an early age, I had to fend for myself, so I experienced some things that a child should not experience, like cold, hunger, neglect, humiliation, etc. However, as a young child, I didn't realize that my living conditions were harsh until I visited my grandparents, aunt, and cousin in California. They were living large in comfort and wealth; at least, that's what I thought. Nevertheless, they were living better than me.

Seeing that was the first time, I can remember being envious, jealous, and sad. My cousin was an only child, and she was spoiled and boastful. Everything was mine, mine, mine with her, and I was not used to that because I had ten siblings, and we had to share. Anyway, when I came home from California, my family moved from the old house to a new house in a new neighborhood. The neighborhood changed, but the living conditions were the same. However, I was now aware that we were considered poor. It was as though a light bulb came on. The hand-me-down clothes, the cold winters, the hot summers, and the empty refrigerator were all because we were poor.

Anyway, I was born into the struggle. I just didn't know it. However, the real struggle for me began when I became a parent and cared about what happened in the world. Crisis and hatred seemed to be rampant and on the move. Because of my children, I wanted to pray. Throughout my life, I struggled with religion because I was introduced to it as a very young child by my mom, grandparents, and the most beautiful older cousin-in-law. I loved the good stories that she read to me, but as time went on, I strayed from her, and worldly life prevailed. Hence, the struggle with good and evil, right and wrong, and love and hate has been a lifelong plight.

In most cases, if we don't know the blessing or value of what we have been given, we abuse or take advantage of it. When I was a child, I grew up in a poor neighborhood, but I was happy. It wasn't until I ventured out into the world that I became envious, jealous, and sad when I saw people living better than me. It has taken me a lifetime to be happy with my blessings, my trials, my lot, and my life. I still struggle, but by the grace of Allah (swt), I am reminded to be thankful and appreciative for my life and not value my worth according to the world but by the love of Allah (swt).

Bism Allah Al-Rahman Al-Rahim

This Struggle Is Real

This struggle is real. Hatred and envy, I feel in my heart. Help me, **Allah Ar Raheem,** I'm falling apart.

This struggle is real. My bones, **the weight of the stress,** is in my back. Guide me, Allah Ar-Rasheed; this anger is leading me off track.

This struggle is real. Words keep **spewing** off my tongue. Stop me, Allah Al-Jabbar, because what I say is **heard by my young.**

This struggle is real. Crazy thoughts, **I visualize** in my head. Humble me, Allah Al-Muzil, because if it were left to me, **those who cross me would all be dead.**

This struggle is real. People, places, and things **will make us forget** our deen. So, if we feel **our nafs** getting the best of us, we must practice what the Qur'an has taught us to do: sincerely seek refuge with Allah Al-Muta'Ali. **For Allah, Malik-Ul-Mulk** is always there **to answer our call.**

Recommended Reading:

- Surah 2 Al-Baqarah Ayats 155-157
- Surah 8 Al Anfāl Ayats 27-29

Wonders of a Treasure Trove to Allah

- Surah 64 At-Taghabun Ayats 14-18
- Surah 57 Al-Hadid Ayats 20-25
- Surah 49 Al-Hujurāt Ayats 6-15
- Surah 27 An-Naml 59-79
- Surah 10 Yūnus Ayats 40-44
- Surah 9 At-Taubah Ayats 23-24

Bism Allah Al-Rahman Al-Rahim

This World

This **world** is such an ugly, lonely, destructive place. Why must my body occupy this space?

I was born to worship Allah (swt) and be tested. So, I am told. What happened **before** to my soul?

The birds, trees, mountains, and seas are such wonders. My life, I dream, sit, and ponder.

Yet, **man is the cause**: the pollution, the violence, and **all** its flaws.

This world is such an ugly, lonely, destructive place. Why must my body occupy this space?

My eyes and ears have seen and heard so many atrocities. **Give me understanding,** please!

My life, I dream, sit, and wonder. What is going to destroy this earth, the solar winds or man's worst blunder?

Beauty without ugliness, its value could never be known. Paradise without hell would never have been cherished. Because of Allah's **wisdom** and **mercy, all humanity will not perish.**

Wonders of a Treasure Trove to Allah

Recommended Reading:

- Surah 15 Al-Hijr Ayats 85-99
- Surah 16 An-Nahl Ayats 79-81
- Surah 10 Yūnus Ayats 24-58*
- Surah 10 Yūnus Ayats 99-103
- Surah 2 Al-Baqarah Ayats 155-157*
- Surah 7 Al-A'rāf Ayat 170
- Surah 67 Al-Mulk Ayats 1-2
- Surah 30 Ar-Rūm Ayats 41-45*

Bism Allah Al-Rahman Al-Rahim

Forgive Me

Forgive me Allah (swt) for asking questions of you. My heart is heavy, and my soul is too.

My sister has been killed. **My son-in-law** has been killed. **The innocent and weak** are being killed. I feel for this. My heart was not built.

I try my best to understand the plan, but they are still dropping bombs on children, women, and men.

This suffering seems sometimes too hard for me to bear. My feeling of helplessness makes me think it would be easier if I didn't care.

Prophecy is that the world will end, **but why must it be so much suffering from the garden till then?**

Forgive me Allah (swt) for asking questions of you, but like the angels, I have questions and we both have been given very few clues.

Your plan and wisdom are yours' alone, **but I truly wonder** what was the entire conversation about mankind's creation upon your throne?

Survival of the fittest, in most cases, refers to the animal kingdom, but mankind's cruelty towards one another makes one wonder **which species is the greater, mankind or the other.**

The angels' question was about the bloodshed. **My question**, if the heavens, earth and mountains refused the test, what in mankind's **DNA** honored us as if we knew best to accept this duress?

Are we the species of Divine Law to answer the questions for all?

Your repentance, mercy, love, and justice; are they the subjects that were discussed?

Which makes me still wonder about the entire conversation upon your throne. **Was Hell and Paradise created for mankind and jinn alone?**

I wonder and ponder about creation as you told me to do, but I just can't figure it out. Believe me, you, in you Allah (swt), my belief is not in doubt.

Your love, mercy, grace, **and justice** have filled my heart, and from you, **I don't ever want to part.**

I love and worship you, Lord, no matter what I go through. **I am just really sad and hurt** to see what mankind do.

Forgive me Allah (swt) for asking questions of you.
This world is a test. I know that we all must go through.

Your plan and your wisdom are yours' alone. **Please, please, please let Paradise be our home.**

Recommended Reading:

- Surah 33 Al-Ahzāb Ayats 60-73*
- Surah 7 Al-A'rāf Ayats 177-188*
- Surah 32 Al-Sajdah Ayats 2-22***
- Surah 38 Sād Ayats 27-29 & 65-88**
- Surah 64 At-Taghaban Ayats 1-18
- Surah 37 Al-Saffāt Ayats 1-43
- Surah 72 Al-Jinn Ayats 1-29*
- Surah 48 Al-Fath Ayats 4-29**
- Surah 2 Al-Baqarah Ayats 28-33 & 82-86
- Surah 55 Ar-Rahmān Ayats 7-78*
- Surah 59 Al-Hashir Ayats 18-24
- Surah 30 Ar-Rūm Ayats 30-45

Bism Allah Al-Rahman Al-Rahim

Limited Understanding

My vile, envious thoughts have limited understanding of the vastness of your love, mercy, your throne, and Kersey.

I clam at the thought of **one having more or better than me.** I am constantly combating this urge. Please set me free!

My being is but a drop in the ocean. Yet, your love for me exemplifies devotion.

Billions, millions, hundreds of years of creation, totally beyond my comprehension. But above all, **you have made me worthy of mentioning.**

My vile, envious thoughts, Allah (swt), how and when will we truly part?

I'm begging you for mercy and forgiveness, too. Because of these thoughts, I feel I'm disappointing you.

I thank you, Allah (swt). **My actions don't match my thoughts.** I am working daily **to keep them apart.**

My limited understanding is coming to the realization that I need not be envious of anyone because You, Allah, Azzawajall, are able and capable of **love for everyone!**

Recommended Reading:

- Surah 8 Al-Anfāl Ayats 22-24*
- Surah 2 Baqarah Ayats 28-32 & 177*
- Surah 57 Al-Hadid Ayats 7-13*
- Surah 45 Al-Jāthiyah Ayats 12-15*
- Surah 39 Az-Zumar Ayats 9-18**
- Surah 71 Nūh Ayats 10-20
- Surah 17 Bani Isra'il Ayat 70*
- Surah 6 Al-An'ām Ayats 50-62*

Wonders of a Treasure Trove to Allah

Bism Allah Al-Rahman Al-Rahim

How Do You Know

Allah (swt) is worthy to be praised! He is Al-Khaliq, my Creator; Al-Muhaymin, my protector; Al-Razzaq, my provider. I love Allah (swt), and I seek His pleasure in all that I do. But how do we know when our deeds are for Allah (swt)?

I **worship** Allah (swt) alone because I want **Paradise** to be my home.

I **fast** because it is mandatory, but I would rather read the Qur'an and other stories.

I **give zakat** because that is something I should do, but it makes me feel good, too.

I **offer salat** to communicate with Allah (swt). I get to keep the line open so He can hear my calls.

Some deeds I like and some deeds I don't, but what does that mean? It remains to be seen.

It seems no matter what I do, I, **myself**, will benefit too.

There are some who praise Allah (swt) **just for show.** You can best believe, Allah (swt) already knows.

Allah's right upon His slave is to worship Allah (swt) and no other, and the slave's right upon Allah (swt) is not to be punished if he answers the call.

So, we should **be sincere** and do the best we can to follow the Qur'an and Sunnah because it is only to Allah (swt) that we must be true.

Recommended Reading:

- Surah 3 Al-Imran Ayat 195
- Surah 53 An-Najm Ayats 30-33
- Surah 39 Az-Zumar Ayats 9-18 & 37-39
- Surah 16 An-Nahl Ayat 125
- Surah 2 Al-Baqarah Ayats 6-15
- Surah 107 Al-Mā'ūn Ayats 1-7
- Sahih Al Bukhari Vol 9 Hadith 470
- Sahih Al Bukhari Vol 1 Hadith 38

Wonders of a Treasure Trove to Allah

Bism Allah Al-Rahman Al-Rahim

My Heart

Thank you, Allah (swt), for **soothing my heart.** You protect my mind from these **crazy** thoughts.

Is it my heart **or** my thoughts that I should be more concerned about? Sometimes, **I am so confused that** I just want to shout.

My heart is sympathetic, loving, and caring, **but** my mind is vengeful, wavering, and scary.

Is it me, O Lord, who thinks this way, or is it Shaytan trying to sway me his way?

I wonder and ponder on this thought a lot. I thank you, Allah (swt), **for reminding me** of what Shaytan **wished I had forgotten.**

Shaytan's whispers are defenseless against your repenting servant. Repentance is what You have given us to ward off that serpent.

My heart, Allah (swt), I gave to you a long time ago. Surely, by the repentance of my forefather, Prophet Adam (as), this Shaytan already knows.

Prophet Adam (as) repented soon after his fall. He knew then that Allah (swt) was the only One to whom he should call.

So, I thank you, Allah (swt), for soothing my heart. I think the heart is **more** powerful than the thought.

Recommended Reading:

- Surah 22 Al-Hajj Ayats 46 & 52-54
- Surah 28 Al-Qasas Ayats 67-70
- Surah 47 Muhammad Ayats 24-39
- Surah 25 Al-Furqān Ayats63-77
- Surah 50 Qāf Ayats 16-34
- Surah 7 Al-A'rāf Ayats 200-206
- Surah 58 Al-Mujadalah Ayats 16-22
- Surah 13 Ar-Ra'd Ayats 26-30

Bism Allah Al-Rahman Al-Rahim

I Still Weep

You have comforted me, Lord, but I still weep. Humanity and its morality are like slaughtering sheep.

The **babies,** my Lord, how can I not cry? The hateful and cruel are causing them to die.

You have comforted me, Lord, but I still weep. Pollution and extinction are killing what is in the ocean's deep.

Ligers, tigons, and bears, **oh my**, are now being crossbred and mixed-bred. For what reason, **I ask why?**

You have comforted me, Lord, but I still weep. Global warming, space travel, artificial intelligence, could it be man's final leap?

Refugees, homeless, fatherless, and motherless, too, their pain is my pain. **I feel it in my heart.** I do!

You have comforted me, Lord, **but I still weep**. I thank you, Allah (swt), for instilling in me compassion, love, and humanity to feed the poor and help the needy too. Worship, I pray that **I will always do.**

Recommended Reading:

- Surah 4 An-Nisā Ayats 115-122*
- Surah 81 At-Takwir Ayats 8-9
- Surah 93 Ad-Duhā Ayats 1-11*
- Surah 92 Al-Lail Ayats 1-7
- Surah 90 Al-Balad Ayats 1-20*
- Surah 76 Ad-Dahr Ayats 5-21
- Surah 63 Al-Munafiqun Ayats 9-11*
- Surah 24 An-Nūr Ayats 18-22
- Surah 30 Ar-Rūm Ayats 30-38*
- Surah 2 Al-Baqarah Ayat 177*

Wonders of a Treasure Trove to Allah

Bism Allah Al-Rahman Al-Rahim

It's Okay

Life can be hard. From the womb, you are already scared.

Your **Momma** and **Daddy** were addicts. You were born with disabilities and panic.

It's okay to cry, but remember Allah (swt) is merciful and loving and always there and on whom we can rely.

Your only child was killed, shot 18 times. But because it was the police who shot him, it was not considered a crime.

It's okay to cry, but remember Allah (swt) is all seeing and knowing, and always there, and on whom we can rely.

Your spouse you love so much that you disowned your family and friends to feel their touch. But what is done in the dark comes out in the light. When you found them sleeping with **your best friend,** you were so ready to end their life.

It's okay to cry, but remember Allah (swt) is all forgiving and pardoning and always there and on whom we can rely.

You were comfortable and living well, and there was no

fault of your own, but bombs just started dropping from the air. You wonder if anyone, if anyone, if anyone cares.

It's okay to cry. Allah (swt) is in control. Some of these horrors have already been foretold.

People of the world don't believe the prophecies to be true, but for the believer, prophecies are important clues.

Clues that can lead us to Heaven's door. Heaven is a place where we won't have to deal with trials anymore.

It's okay to cry, but no matter what the devastation, we must keep believing and living, and on Allah (swt) we must rely.

Recommended Reading:

- Surah 41 Ha Mim Al-Sajdah Ayats 47-54
- Surah 42 Ash-Shūra Ayats 11-21
- Surah 2 Al-Baqarah Ayats 155-157
- Surah 29 Al-'Ankabūt Ayats 2-14
- Surah 57 Al-Hadid Ayats 20-25
- Surah 7 Al-A'rāf Ayats 200-206

Bism Allah Al-Rahman Al-Rahim

Why Me

It is hard to pay a criminal **for what Allah (swt) has already given**, but that is what some people must do, depending on what country or region they live in.

Bandits and criminals, you pass by every day, **hoping** they don't notice you as you go on your way.

Fear is a motivator to do right or wrong, **but the believer won't put up with bad behavior for long.**

You look to the heavens and ask, **why me?** We are all born for a purpose, and only Allah (swt) knows our destiny.

Death is for sure for all who are born. Blessed be the person who fulfills their purpose and weathers the storms.

Pain and suffering are felt all around the world. Vengeance is the Lord's and upon those who wreak havoc and on whom Allah (swt) chooses to destroy.

You walk the earth trying to do right and be right, but you constantly find yourself having to fight.

You look to the heavens and ask, **why me?** However, **you are now calling and closer to Allah (swt),** the One and only true God, than ever before. These trials have got your attention, that is for sure.

Unfortunately, it took your life to be shook, but your patience and perseverance Allah (swt) will never overlook.

Recommended Reading:

- Surah 41 Ha Mim Al-Sajdah Ayats 47-54
- Surah 47 Muhammad Ayats 1-7
- Surah 48 Al-Fath Ayats 1-16
- Surah 49 Al-Hujurāt Ayats 14-18
- Surah 2 Al-Baqarah Ayats 155-157
- Surah 29 Al-'Ankabūt Ayats 2-14
- Surah 57 Al-Hadid Ayats 20-25

Bism Allah Al-Rahman Al-Rahim

It's Me

It's me, O Lord, **I am crying again.** I failed the test we talked about and committed a sin.

I am beating myself up about being weak. Help me through this pain for it is Your love I seek.

I feel like such a failure that I let my nafs get the best of me. So, I tried to find comfort in what the lesson was to be.

My only consolation is at least I tried, **but I am humiliated and disgusted with all this pride.**

I've been begging You to humble me, and You definitely know what to do because the tests and trials are really something tough to go through.

They say to be careful of what you ask for. If it humbles me, **I have no regrets** because Paradise is where I want to rest.

So, I keep on trying to be that servant. **I thank You for allowing me to be able to repent.**

Repentance your gift of eternity. I pray **Paradise** is my reality.

Recommended Reading:

- Surah 49 Al-Hujurāt Ayats 14-18
- Surah 2 Al-Baqarah Ayats 155-157
- Surah 29 Al-'Ankabūt Ayats 2-14
- Surah 25 Al-Furqān Ayats 63-76
- Surah 7 Al-A'rāf Ayats 200-206
- Surah 76 Ad-Dahr Ayats 1-22

Bism Allah Al-Rahman Al-Rahim

The Rope

Oh Allah (swt), **please extend me the rope** so I can hope.

Forty years is a **very long time** for a crime I did not commit. By my hands, I sit and wonder, what could I have done to make these prison gates a 40-year blunder?

My youth, **Oh Lord,** has passed me by. As a believer, I shall not cry.

I **changed** my life, thinking, and disposition. Islam has become **my greatest mission.**

The rope, I need it so I can hope. **Your servant** is begging for mercy to cope.

I'm reaching and grasping for just a sign. **Please, Allah (swt), let it be my time!**

Extend to me the **same rope** you extended to Prophet Ibrahim (as) when you brought him out of the fire, Prophet Yusuf (as) out of prison, Prophet Job (as) out of his misery, **and to all, you granted victory.**

Although I am not a prophet, **to your worship,** I am

trying to be a steadfast servant.

Please extend the same rope to me so **I, too can hope.**

Recommended Reading:

- Surah 3 Al-Imran Ayat 102-104*
- Surah 8 Al-Anfāl Ayat 24-29*
- Surah 48 Al Fath Ayats 1-5
- Surah 42 Ash-Shūrā Ayat 25-28
- Surah 28 Al-Qasa Ayats 9-13*
- Surah 41 HaMim Al-Sajdah/Fussilat Ayats 30-32
- Surah 2 Al-Baqarah Ayats 155-157
- Surah 37 As-Saffāt Ayats 75-82*
- Surah 93 Ad-Duhā Ayats 1-11*
- Surah 29 Al Ankabūt Ayats 24-26

Bism Allah Al-Rahman Al-Rahim

No Reason

When we **know** Allah (swt) is the **One** and **Only God** to be true. We have **no reason** to be blue.

The hard times are good. The good times are better as long as we practice our deen to the letter.

After hardship comes ease, after hardship comes ease, **one hardship**, two ease, Allah (swt) always does **more to please.**

No reason to fear; Allah (swt) sends angels to protect our sphere, front, sides, and rear.

The impossible **becomes** possible. The dubious is clear. No matter what the situation, **Allah (swt)** is always there.

No reason to feel distressed, for anger, sorrow, sadness, and strife are all part of life.

After hardship comes ease, after hardship comes ease, one hardship, **two ease,** Allah (swt) always does **more to please!**

Recommended Reading:

- Surah 4 An-Nisā Ayat 170
- Surah 15 Al-Hijr Ayats 85-88
- Surah 8 Al-Anfāl Ayats 24-30
- Surah 10 Yūnus Ayats 3-10
- Surah 65 At-Talāq Ayats 7-12
- Surah 94 Al-Inshirāh Ayats 1-8*

My Epitome 3

Things that glitter, that are big, that are new, that are pretty grasp our attention. The eyes are so powerful. This is why Islam teaches us to lower our gaze. Once you see something, especially haram, you can't unsee it. Our eyes are cameras, a gift from Allah (swt). The first look is permissible, but the second look is from the whispers of Shaytan.

He whispers, "Look and look again, for it is delightful." The eyes have now penetrated the heart, the heart has penetrated the mind, and the mind has penetrated the hands, feet, tongue, and other body parts in a matter of seconds. From seeing, you have now entered the realm of good and evil, right and wrong, love and hate. Your eyes have caused you to have to make a decision. All the while, Shaytan whispers about the wrong decision.

You have a guardian angel as well advising for good, but if your iman is weak, your desires will get the best of you. So, we must stay prayed up, seek refuge in Allah (swt) every day, morning, noon, and night, and pray our five obligatory prayers. Otherwise, our lives will be a ball of confusion, torment, depression, and imprisonment, similar to hell on earth.

Then there is the hereafter. The eyes are powerful, and

thus we should lower our gaze. Avoid taking a second look. Run from temptation. Don't indulge in bad company. Follow not the footsteps of Shaytan, for Shaytan is an open enemy to mankind.

Bism Allah Al-Rahman Al-Rahim

Open Enemy

Shaytan once was a favorite of Allah (swt), **but when the command came to submit to Adam (as), he refused** to answer our **Master's call.**

Speaking with Shaytan, **Allah (swt) gave him every opportunity to repent.** However, **pride** and **envy** manifested itself, and **Shaytan became arrogant.**

An atom's weight of pride, Shaytan acted as if it were overrated. **Repentance** would have been better for the fire as **he would be forever slated.**

He vowed to **attack man** from front, behind, left, and right using future desires, past experiences, self-worth, and holiness to confuse man about his true plight.

Shaytan is of the world of the unseen. However, his presence is seen and felt throughout the heavens and universe. His destruction and atrocities continue to get worse.

So much of humanity don't believe. The **soul of man** is what Shaytan is seeking to retrieve.

Shaytan comes **to steal, kill, and destroy** because he

regrets that he **underestimated Allah's knowledge** of whom and what Allah (swt) created.

Allah (swt) is the Master, Supreme, Creator of us and everything. **None gets to refuse Allah's demands,** commands, or calls. **None!**

Recommended Reading:

- Surah 2 Al-Baqarah Ayats 34-36
- Surah 2 Al-Baqarah Ayat 98*
- Surah 36 Yā-Sin Ayats 58-66
- Surah 38 Sād Ayats 71-85*
- Surah 17 Al-Isrā Ayats 61-65*
- Surah 16 An-Nahl Ayat 22-23
- Surah 21 Al-Anbiyā' ayat 23*
- Surah 24 An-Nūr Ayat 21*
- Surah 7 Al-A'rāf Ayats 16-17 & 27*
- Surah 39 Az-Zumar Ayats 62-72*

Bism Allah Al-Rahman Al-Rahim

The Veil

And what will let us know what the veil is? It is the present-day punishment of Allah (swt) for the drama and mayhem we cause with our own hands, which can lead us to our downfall.

Prophet Muhammad (saw)**, the last and final messenger,** has been sent but people refuse to answer his call to repent.

Following bad behavior, sin, and shirk, too, **they then boast** to bring on the punishment **if the message is true.**

Actions of people throughout the history of time to now. We can't blame Allah (swt) **for the veil** if **we refuse to bow.**

Eyes and heart **veils have been placed over** because the people follow their forefathers on conjecture: **opinions or guesses based on little or no evidence.** Yet, the Qur'an, **its signs,** even scientists are becoming convinced.

Fortunately, **Allah (swt) is merciful** to all who sincerely repent. So, we should **choose wisely** whom we follow and whom we **represent.**

Recommended Reading:

- Surah 4 An-Nisā Ayats 164-173*
- Surah 36 Yā-Sin Ayats 6-12*
- Surah 53 An-Najm Ayats 23-33*
- Surah 10 Yūnus Ayat 36 & 66*
- Surah 45 Al-Jāthiyah Ayats 23-37*
- Surah 39 Az-Zumar 23-27*
- Surah 24 An-Nūr 18-22*
- Surah 22 Al-Hajj 8-14 & 72-78
- Surah 25 Al-Furqān Ayats 27-34*
- Surah 26 Ash-Shu'rā 70-104*

Wonders of a Treasure Trove to Allah

Bism Allah Al-Rahman Al-Rahim

Coward

Be the man you were born to be. I didn't say raised because maybe your Momma and Daddy didn't care, but you know wrong from right because Allah (swt) gave **you** that insight, coward!

You're out here slinging dope, hitting your girl, and making your Momma cry. **BOY**, it is easy to die, but it is harder to live, coward!

You won't go get a real job because that would take nerve. Something you don't have and don't even deserve, coward!

You run around strapped, creating mischief and havoc. But when you go down, you **weep, squeal, and panic,** coward!

You kill innocent children and bystanders who get caught up in your mess, and for the brothers who accept and encourage this behavior, Allah (swt) willing, the **Hellfire** is where you all will rest, coward!

Some vile, degraded human being thought killing the whole family was cool, and you jumped on **his bandwagon. You are such a fool,** coward!

Allah (swt) commanded an **eye for an eye.** You need to **READ** the word because that thing you call street justice is not what you really heard, coward!

You run around wondering who the snitch is! You betrayed Allah; that is the **GREATEST SIN** of them all, coward!

A real man would try to walk away, but if a situation must go down, he would not jeopardize everyone around; coward!

I can go on and on with this mess, but **let me get to my point and put this to rest!**

Shaytan will have you believe that the **Hellfire** is not real and that this is the only life you get to live. Well, you can best believe **that fire gets hot,** and you will keep on burning to beget what you begot.

If you don't repent now and death comes knocking at your door, you're going to wish you didn't have all those evil deeds in store.

Instead of gin and juice, you're going to be made to drink boiling, festering water, screaming for the gatekeepers to quench your thirst. They're going to ask, **did you put Allah (swt) first?**

Your skin will keep burning and melting away, only to come back again and again. At that time, you will long for death, **but** it is Allah (swt) who you crossed, so He will never take your breath.

What you don't realize is that when you attack me, you attack Allah (swt). When you attack your brethren, you attack Allah (swt). When you attack society, you attack Allah (swt). This is Allah's creation; it is not yours. Unto Allah (swt) is the final return, so do good to better your score because the angels are watching and recording, too. **This is not the only life you have to go through.**

If you are going to be a coward, be a COWARD for Allah (swt). Fear His signs, words, punishment, and it all. Teach the brothers not to take Allah's words as a joke because when all is said and done, you are going to wish you had spoke, coward!

Recommended Reading:

- Surah 17 Al Isra Ayats 33-43*
- Surah 40 Al-Ghāfir Ayats 47-52**
- Surah 39 Az-Zumar Ayats 52-59*
- Surah 30 Luqmān Ayats 11-26**
- Surah 35 Fātir Ayats 36-40*
- Surah 19 Maryam Ayats 71-72*
- Surah 42 Ash-Shūra Ayats 39-48*
- Surah 3 Al-Imran Ayats 30-34
- Surah 2 Al-Baqarah Ayats 165-167& 79*

- Surah 5 Al-Māidah Ayats 45 & 79*
- Surah 4 An-Nisā 135*

Wonders of a Treasure Trove to Allah

Bism Allah Al-Rahman Al-Rahim

You Thief

Beware of what you do. Mesmerizing the weak and vulnerable mind by telling it **to just do you. Forgetting about Allah's commands and laws.** Portraying them as if they are flaws.

The talent and the gift Allah (swt) bestowed upon you. You lure the innocent and the confused **all so you can be amused.**

You and your music acquaintance are constantly competing in the name of egotistical competition and putting on ostentatious displays of wealth at the expense of the brokenhearted, the wayward from whom you profit, **but they are left Godless.**

There is **no limit** to your schemes, **and you often** use Shaytan as a means.

You think you are doing good, but that is only a mirage because you cannot tell people **to just do you** because then you are telling them to forget about God.

You steal their fear. You make them think they don't have to care.

But when they stand before Allah (swt), **their burdens you cannot bear.**

Beware of what you take, **you thief,** because there is a severe punishment for someone's belief!

Repent and stop selling your soul. Allah (swt) is the only one who can fill your empty void and make you whole.

Recommended Reading:

- Surah 68 Al-Qalam Ayats 35-52*
- Surah 37 Al-Saffāt Ayats 22-62**
- Surah 40 Al-Mu'min Ayats 41-55
- Surah 57 Al-Hadid Ayats 20-25
- Surah 2 Al-Baqarah Ayats 261-286
- Surah 52 At-Tūr Ayats 11-21
- Surah 53 An-Najm Ayats 24-62*
- Surah 102 At-Takathur Ayats 1-8
- Surah 71 Nūh Ayats 21-28
- Surah 56 Al-Wāqi'ah Ayats 45-56

Bism Allah Al-Rahman Al-Rahim

Don't Worry

Don't worry about **Hell!** It's okay! You'll come to know it on Resurrection Day!

Don't worry! You believe! This is your only life. Life is all play, and no one can stand in your way.

Malik, the overseer of **Hell,** will meet you at the gate. Get familiar with his name because this is what you chose to be your fate. He'll let you know the fire gets hot, and because of your deeds, you'll never change your lot.

ALLAH (swt) is the MASTER OF TORMENT; the hooks, chains, and furnace are only a few. Allah (swt) has in store torments no one has **EVER** felt or knew.

Prophet Muhammad (saw) **saw these truths** when he went on the night journey. **Unfortunately,** you won't see it until you are lying on the gurney.

ALLAH (swt) blessed the Prophet (saw) with this knowledge to set the people aright so that they would know what **could possibly** be their plight.

Don't worry about **Hell! Malik,** the overseer, won't care if you scream or yell! Allah (swt) created him for this

very purpose, **and he loves it** because it is only to Allah (swt) he must submit.

Recommended Reading:

- Surah 16 An-Nahl Ayats 22 & 29**
- Surah 64 At-Taghabun Ayats 7-18*
- Surah 7 Al-A'rāf Ayats 172-184*
- Surah 74 Al-Muddaththir Ayats 26-56**
- Surah 23 Al-Muminum Ayats 99-106*
- Surah 43 Az-Zukhruf Ayats 74-80**
- Surah 84 Al-Inshiqāq Ayats 1-25**
- Surah 39 Az-Zumar Ayats 52-63*
- Surah 9 At-Taubah Ayat 79-82*
- Surah 26 Ash-Shu'rā Ayats 200-223*
- Surah 15 Al-Hijr Ayats 2-4**
- Surah 67 Al-Mulk Ayats 6-11*
- Surah 40 Al-Mu'Min Ayats 41-55
- Surah 38 Sād Ayats 55-66

Wonders of a Treasure Trove to Allah

Bism Allah Al-Rahman Al-Rahim

Woe

Woe to you, my brother! You're open! You're not undercover!

You're spending **crazy** money and scoping out all the honeys. That is not keeping your sins hid, and you're teaching them to your kids.

Woe! **Your Momma and Daddy needed you.** You were too busy to see to your kin. That work you were doing won't help you in the end.

You got a wife here and a mistress over there. That's not an act of a believer. That is **the act** of the Great Deceiver.

Woe! Stop! **You're caught up!** Go back to being like you were before you got like you are. **Seek Allah (swt)** and ask for mercy, too, because it is only by the grace of Allah (swt) that any of us will make it through.

Recommended Reading:

- Surah 4 An-Nisā Ayats 36-37**
- Surah 4 An-Nisā Ayats 142-148*
- Surah 35 Fātir Ayats 1-7*
- Surah 16 An-Nahl Ayats 45-52*

- Surah 83 At-Tatfif Ayats 1-36**
- Surah 77 Al-Mursalāt Ayats 14-50*
- Surah 75 Al-Qiyāmah Ayats 34-40*
- Surah 62 Al-Jumu'ah Ayats 9-11*
- Surah 39 Az-Zumar Ayats 53-59 & 69-75

Bism Allah Al-Rahman Al-Rahim

Beyond Bounds

Did not Shaytan promise to lure mankind **from the front, back, and sides?** Yet, mankind manipulates and changes **Allah's creation with great pride.**

Did not Shaytan threaten to lead astray and arouse in mankind vain desires? Yet, many of mankind have become cosmetically fake, ordering designer babies. What was **once intended for medicine,** you have made it a craving.

Did not Shaytan threaten to lead mankind to cut the ears of cattle and alter Allah's creation? Yet, mankind allows **gene-altering organizations** to change the molecular design of conception to make a **three-parent baby,** Mommas' baby, Pop Pop's maybe!

Organizations that alter genes in plants, animals, and mankind. The natural process of reproduction in the near future may be hard to find.

Cloning pigs and injecting them **with human cells** for organ use. Allah (swt) forbade the pig, so that is just a case of severe abuse.

Mankind lacks knowledge of what has really been done. **Shaytan is acting as if he has already won.**

Allah (swt) is the only Creator. **What mankind does is manipulate and abuse what Allah (swt) has already created.**

So, those who listen to the whispers of Shaytan, the **Hellfire** is where you all may intertwine.

You have gone beyond bounds and passed the limit. Your confusion, deceptiveness, and artificiality have corrupted humanity, and we don't know what is fake or what is reality.

Recommended Reading:

- Surah 43 Az-Zukhruf Ayats 74-89
- Surah 72 Al-Jinn Ayats 1-15
- Surah 51 Az-Zāriyāt Ayats 1-60
- Surah 45 Al-Jāthiyah Ayats 7-15
- Surah 4 An-Nisā Ayats 115-122
- Surah 56 Al-Wāqi'ah Ayats 57-77

Wonders of a Treasure Trove to Allah

Bism Allah Al-Rahman Al-Rahim

Three Meals and a Pot

Three meals and **a pot,** that's what you chose to be your lot.

The lies you told spread all around the world. Now, you're labeled a liar. **You're playing with fire!**

You didn't have to take my money from me. **You could have asked.** I know it was you under that mask.

"You're playing with fire!" I holler. That money you stole will be your collar.

You put your career before Allah (swt), and you didn't answer the Master's call.

You're playing with fire! If you don't change, I have no doubt! It will be a funky smell when the angels rip your soul out.

Three meals and a pot, that's what you chose to be your lot. Drink the boiling, festering water. There are no meals in **Hell** that you can place to order. Eat from the Zaqqum tree and devour the pus that oozes from sores. That is all you will eat. You can rest assured. Now that the **pot is hot,** you can pick what you think is the **very best spot.**

Recommended Reading:

- Surah 14 Ibrāhim Ayats 1-7
- Surah 2 Al-Baqarah Ayats 267- 268*
- Surah 37 As-Saffāt Ayats 62-68*
- Surah 16 An-Nahl Ayats 45-52 & 85*
- Surah 9 At-Taubah Ayats 79-82 *
- Surah 39 Az-Zumar Ayats 69-75*
- Surah 19 Maryan Ayat 66-84*
- Surah 77 Al-Mursalāt Ayats 28-40 *
- Surah 38 Sād Ayats 55-65*
- Surah 44 Ad-Dukhan Ayats 43-51*

Bism Allah Al-Rahman Al-Rahim

Sins of the Heart

Seeing and knowing you're beautiful, wealthy, wise, or intelligent are not sins, **but boasting, looking down,** or **abusing others** because of it will lead you to the **Hellfire Pit!**

Scoffing and turning your back on the poor and needy all because **you believe** them to be unworthy and greedy.

Rejecting people because of how they look. **Evidently,** you have not read Allah's book.

Haughtiness and arrogance are sins. Sins of the heart, they are by far.

Lust, wrath, envy, pride, sloth, gluttony, and greed are **characteristics one should shun** without a doubt indeed.

Follow not the footsteps of Shaytan, humble thyself, and **relinquish that pride. Allah (swt)** is who we want to be **our GOD.**

Recommended Reading:

- Surah 7 Al-A'rāf Ayat 186
- Surah 7 Al-A'rāf Ayats 205-206

- Surah 8 Al-Anfāl Ayats 36-37
- Surah 16 An-Nahl Ayats 37-40
- Surah 16 An-Nahl Ayats 95-100
- Surah 68 Al-Qalam Ayats 7-16
- Surah 53 An-Najm Ayats 33-42
- Surah 23 Al-Mu'minum Ayats 62-69
- Surah 73 Al-Muzzammil 8-15
- Surah 113 Al-Falaq Ayats 1-5
- Surah 102 At-Takathur Ayats 1-8
- Surah 25 Al-Furqān Ayat 43
- Surah 24 An-Nūr Ayat 26*

Bism Allah Al-Rahman Al-Rahim

Don't Get Angry

Don't get angry! Don't get angry! Don't get angry. Words of wisdom if I must speak frankly!

However, anger finds its way into my heart. **When I see what goes on in this world, bullies brutally beating down a girl.**

Mass shootings in schools are manifested **because society lacks rules.**

Same-sex marriages, and now they want a man and a man with a baby carriage.

Pandemics and diseases are everywhere, yet **man is disrespectful** of it and shows no fear.

War and genocide are on the move. History repeats itself if nothing improves.

Forces of evil are unseen. **People don't understand why** they have the desire to be so mean.

Allah (swt) says in the Qur'an, stand up for righteousness **even if it is against your own kin.** Shaytan doesn't care about relationships because he knows the fire is his end.

Shaytan, **the great deceiver,** comes to steal, kill, and destroy. He has an army of **jinns, and he is their envoy.**

But don't despair about the power of Allah (swt). For when it is time for battle, and at times battle is a necessity, **Allah (swt) sends angels to fight for and with you and me.**

So don't get angry! Don't get angry! Don't get angry! **Allah (swt)** is the King of kings, Creator of worlds, Master of life and death. He provides for us. He slays for us. When **Allah (swt)** decrees, **Shaytan will have no breath!**

Recommended Reading:

- Surah 2 Al-Baqarah Ayat 255-2588
- Surah 3 Al-Imran Ayats 132-135
- Surah 3 Al-Imran Ayat 159
- Surah 8 Al-Anfāl Ayats 15-30 * 52-59
- Surah 4 An-Nisā Ayat 135*
- Surah 17 Al-Isrā' Ayats 61-65
- Surah 23 Al-Mu'minum Ayat 94-118**
- Sahih Al-Bukhari 6114

Bism Allah Al-Rahman Al-Rahim

Death

Creep, Creep, Creep, death is knocking at the door. It has claimed one brother, two brothers, and more.

Like the wind, it is blowing through, whispering furiously to some and calmly to others. **Stop!** You shall **breathe no further.**

Man really has **no concept** of death's meaning: the finality, the questions, and the screening.

If he did, he wouldn't laugh and **talk vile** at the grave site. **The dead can hear.** Allah (swt) gave them that right.

The body is **forever no more,** but the soul is able to soar.

From Allah (swt), we came, and unto Allah (swt), we must return; our good deeds, our bad deeds, a total of what we earned.

Laugh now, weep later for all who **don't think death is greater.**

Greater than fame, sex, money, women, and men because **a battle against death we will never win!**

Recommended Reading:

- Surah 15 Al-Hijr Ayats 86-94**
- Surah 16 An-Nahl Ayats 33-37&45-52**
- Surah 53 An-Najm Ayats 42-44**
- Surah 39 Az-Zumar Ayats 53-59 **
- Surah 37 As-Saffāt Ayats 22-74**
- Surah 32 As-Sajdah Ayats 9-13*
- Surah 29 Al-'Ankabūt Ayats 56-58 &2-7 **
- Surah 23 Al-Mu'minum Ayats 99-106*
- Surah 9 At-Taubah Ayats 79-82*
- Surah 31 Luqmān Ayats 33-34**
- Surah 83 At-Tatfif Ayats 29-36**

My Epitome 4

Allah (swt) has given us free will to choose whom we will worship. However, we never had a choice of who our family would be. We didn't choose our mothers, fathers, sisters, brothers, cousins, aunts, uncles, etc. We didn't choose the region where we would be born nor the date or time of our birth. Allah (swt) decreed our kin for us and stipulated that we not sever the ties of kinship. So that uncle who takes out his teeth when he eats, you have got to love him and not say much. In some cases, the people who have given birth to us are not the people who raised us. Also, some of us are born into wealth, and others into poverty. The struggle of our lives was determined before we were even born – nothing we did or said. Allah (swt) decreed it.

The reality of it all is the instruction book on how to be good parents is in the word of Allah (swt), but most of us bypass His word and wing it from the start. Out of the gate, we set our families up for chaos.

Family relations are intricate and unique because bonding is based on character, time spent, pecking order, gender, etc. For instance, the first-born child is favored most of the time. Yet, the firstborn is also held responsible for the younger siblings. The male child is favored over the female child, etc. Nevertheless, Allah (swt) blessed mankind with mercy, so love binds mother and daughter, father and son, sister and brother, etc. We love our families, and we would die for them – at least some of us and for some of them. Family are the people who can hurt us the most because of the bond that we have with them. Also, we have friends that we treat as family, and we allow ourselves to get pulled into their schemes, lies, and drama, and their drama compounded upon our own drama, which leads to chaos.

We devote our loyalty to kin and not to Allah (swt). Allah (swt) says in the Qur'an to stand up for justice even if it is against your own kin. Again, if we don't follow the word of Allah (swt), we invite chaos in our lives. So, say no when it is necessary and yes when it is warranted, and don't sever the ties of kinship. Just draw the line, putting Allah (swt) foremost.

Bism Allah Al-Rahman Al-Rahim

My Lifeline

My life had taken such a toll. **I thought** I would never get old. But my God, conscious of my lifeline to Adam (as) and Eve (as), reminded me that **my soul was only for Allah (swt) to retrieve.**

In my weakest moment, my deepest despair, **Allah (swt) sent you, my son,** so I could care.

I thank Allah (swt) for you every day. Because of you, I want to pray.

You are **my firstborn, my only son, my lifeline!**

Recommended Reading:

- Surah 2 Al-Baqarah Ayat 45
- Surah 7 Al A'rāf Ayats 172 & 187**
- Surah 9 At-Taubah 19-23
- Surah 16 An-Nahl Ayat 78
- Surah 52 At-Tūr Ayats 21-28
- Surah 46 Al-Ahqaf Ayats 15-16**
- Surah 31 Luqmān Ayats 13-19*
- Surah 14 Ibrāhim Ayat 37-41*
- Surah 25 Al-Furqān Ayats 74-75

Bism Allah Al-Rahman Al-Rahim

Habibah

Oh Habibah, my beloved, Allah (swt) has blessed me and sent you from above.

Brokenhearted and shattered, **I cut my birth cord.** But little did I know in my daughter, you were stored.

I **saw you** in my dream for so many nights. **It put my mind and body** in such an ugly fight.

Allah forgave me for my sin. I know this when I see you grin.

I pray your journey in life will make you someone's **happy wife.**

People look high and low. For what, they don't even know.

Our first and foremost purpose is Allah (swt). In Him, we can have love, trust, and it all.

Don't let anyone belittle you for being a happy wife. For, **truthfully,** they would rather have your life.

Oh Habibah, my beloved, **my final note from me to**

you, so listen carefully and take heed too. Although our husbands are our only boo, **Allah (swt) should always come first and foremost to you.**

Recommended Reading:

- Surah 15 Al-Hijr Ayats 2-3
- Surah 66 At-Tahrim Ayats 1-12
- Surah 9 At-Taubah Ayats 23-24
- Surah 24 An-Nūr Ayats 31-53
- Surah 14 Ibrāhim Ayat 3

Bism Allah Al-Rahman Al-Rahim

Momma Knows

Your children you bore of your own brought children for you to feed from other homes.

You may have complained a little here and a little there, **but** when you knew their situations, you endured because you cared.

Your **kindness, your love,** and **sympathy** have got you through. Allah (swt) has been watching and blessing you.

I watched you shop, cook, clean, and chastise. **It is because of you that I am so wise.**

You and **your families** have been the world to me. How much, I don't think any of you know, but because of you, I'm watching my grandchildren grow.

Momma Knows, Momma Knows, Momma Knows.

I lost my mom a long time ago, but **you all** filled that void, **indeed! I hope you all know!**

Recommended Reading:

- Surah 57 Al-Hadid Ayats 18-19 & 27
- Surah 93 Ad-Duhā Ayats 1-11

Wonders of a Treasure Trove to Allah

- Surah 99 Az-Zilzal Ayats 7-8
- Surah 4 An-Nisā Ayat 40
- Surah 2 Al-Baqarah Ayat 62
- Surah 17 Bani Isra'il Ayats 18-31
- Surah 11 Hūd Ayat 16

Bism Allah Al-Rahman Al-Rahim

She Calls Herself Niya

She calls herself **Niya,** but that is not her name. **Because of me,** she was so ashamed.

My baby called out to me. But because of my own pain, I couldn't hear or see.

I know I wasn't always right, but Lord, **I had no real idea** of her plight.

She blames me for her issues today. I wish I could take her pain away.

I've apologized. I've turned my life around. No matter what I do, I still see a frown.

Allah (swt) has heard my cries and forgiven me. I told her that it was not up to her to set me free!

I **love** my daughter, that is for sure. **Together, we will seek Allah (swt) as our cure.**

She calls herself **Niya,** and that is okay; you see. Because she will always be an extension of **me!**

Recommended Reading:

- Surah 64 At-Taghabun Ayats 14-18
- Surah 34 As-Saba' Ayats 35-37
- Surah 9 At-Taubah Ayats 22-25*
- Surah 25 Al-Furqān 70-76
- Surah 52 At-Tūr Ayat 21*
- Surah 31 Luqmān Ayats 13-19
- Surah 7 Al'A'rāf Ayats 189-201

Bism Allah Al-Rahman Al-Rahim

From the Womb

I have loved my children from the womb. Little did I know they would change soon.

Early in my pregnancies, **I knew** my children were Allah's gift to me!

But the older they got, the angels they were not.

Motherhood can only be taught to a certain degree because everyone's experiences are different, you see.

Then there is **Daddy,** who you must not forget because **it all can affect your wit.**

I have loved my children from the womb. They were not born with silver spoons.

Times were hard, **and help was few.** It was only by **the grace of Allah (swt) that** we made it through.

After Allah (swt), I credit my children, grandchildren, and my progeny to come for who I am today. Because of them, I changed my way.

I have loved my children from the womb. Allah (swt)

willing, we will be **in PARADISE together after the SWOON.**

Recommended Reading:

- Surah 17 Al-Isrā' Ayat 70 **
- Surah 7 Al-A'rāf Ayats 187-189**
- Surah 35 Fātir Ayat 11*
- Surah 22 Al-Hajj Ayats 1-7*
- Surah 27 An-Naml Ayats 86-89*
- Surah 9 At-Taubah Ayats 23-24*
- Surah 23 Al-Mu'minūn Ayats 12-16*
- Surah 39 Az-Zumar Ayats 68-75**
- Surah 25 Al-Furqān Ayats 74-76*
- Surah 52 At-Tūr Ayats 21-28*

Bism Allah Al-Rahman Al-Rahim

Sister

Assalamu Alaikum! Sister, why won't you greet me back when I greet you? This is what Allah (swt) commanded us to do.

I hope you don't think you're more worthy than me to praise Allah (swt) because Allah (swt) is the CREATOR of us ALL.

There is only one GOD. There should only be one Muslim community, but pride and arrogance have got us all living in hostility.

I may not **look, talk, or dress like you,** but I love Allah (swt). Allah (swt) willing, I will try to do whatever to answer **my Master's call.**

So, turn your head and act like you don't see, but when I greet you, I greet you out of love for Allah (swt). I hope I will always, **always,** answer my Master's call, **Assalamu Alaikum.**

Recommended Reading:

- Surah 4 An-Nisā Ayat 86
- Surah 21 Al-Anbiyā' Ayats 92 & 93

Wonders of a Treasure Trove to Allah

- Surah 22 Al-Hajj Ayats 8 & 9
- Sahih Muslim, Book of Faith Vol 1, Hadith 164
- Surah 10 Yūnus Ayat 10
- Surah 49 Al-Hujurāt Ayat 11*
- Surah 27 An-Naml Ayats 69-82*
- Surah 58 Al-Mujadalah Ayat 22

Regina Woods

Bism Allah Al-Rahman Al-Rahim

It Hurts

It **hurts**, my heart! **Oh Allah (swt)**, the streets done claimed them all!

My son, father, brother and husband, too, are all locked down. **What is a woman to do?**

It hurts, my body! I can't even get out of bed. These crazy thoughts keep running through my head.

I told them Allah (swt). I told them life was not all play, and as a consequence, it could end this way.

It hurts that they didn't listen to me. **Now, we all are in jail, wanting to be free.**

It hurts because I really want to give them a smackdown and abandon them too. But with your guidance, I only lend my support in hopes of seeing them through.

Although this is not what I asked for in life. **Allah (swt) knows best.** Surely, this is a test.

It hurts that the years have gone by. The times I needed them most. I was all alone, and all I could do was cry.

Wonders of a Treasure Trove to Allah

I know Allah (swt). In my deepest despair, I should seek you because you are always there.

It hurts because sometimes I want a body, too, **just to hear the words**, "I am here for you!"

Recommended Reading:

- Surah 2 Al-Baqarah Ayats 155-157
- Surah 9 At-Taubah Ayats 22-25
- Surah 8 Al-Anfāl Ayats 28-29
- Surah 64 At-Taghabun Ayats 11-18
- Surah 57 Al-Hadid Ayats 20-25
- Surah 35 Al-Fātir Ayat 8
- Surah 27 An-Naml Ayats 60-75
- Surah 25 Al-Furqān Ayats 17-20 & 43
- Surah 28 Al-Qasa Ayats 9-13*

Bism Allah Al-Rahman Al-Rahim

WHY?

Why do children ask questions like "Why?" Their inquisitiveness and curiosity are something unique. Something I believe **adults** should seek.

Why do we want to lose weight to impress? We fast, we diet, and we take dope. **Truthfully, without Allah (swt), there is no hope.** We will regress to what we used to know, and all that effort would have been just for show.

Why do our loved ones always wind up **asking for a helping hand** after you tell them not to go that way? But to them, life is nothing but play.

Why do we want what we can't have? **We lie, cheat,** and **steal in WAYS** we know not, just to neglect what we begot.

Why is the **burden** of every serious family situation placed on one particular family member with no invitation? But when money is found, they all come around.

Why do we not seek the truth in a situation? The truth hurts, **but a lie can kill,** especially if you are at the wrong end of the deal.

Wonders of a Treasure Trove to Allah

Why do we do the things we do? I find in me that which I am not. I think for this "**Why,**" **I'll pray a lot.**

So why do children ask questions like "**Why?**" Truthfully, it is simple: **seek, and ye shall find.**

Recommended Reading:

- Surah 16 An-Nahl Ayats 26 & 43-44
- Surah 79 An-Nāzi'āt Ayats 42-46
- Surah 78 An-Naba' Ayats 1-36
- Surah 68 Al-Qalam Ayats 35-44
- Surah 67 Al-Mulk Ayat 6-11
- Surah 61 As-Saff Ayats 1-13
- Surah 52 At-tūr Ayats 29-49
- Surah 41 Ha Mim Al-Sadjah Ayats 9-12
- Surah 35 Fātir Ayats 15-24
- Surah 34 As-Saba' Ayats 25-28

Bism Allah Al-Rahman Al-Rahim

Muslims

The **shield of faith** is more powerful than **any** Goliath. Remember Prophet David (as) slew Goliath by faith, **and we Muslims**, in turn, by faith will be, Insha Allah, triumphant.

Muslims have to account for what is happening to our brothers and sisters around the world.

Our in-fighting, backbiting, and arms against each other we have hurled.

Palestinians, Syrians, Yemenis, Uyghurs, Ethiopians, and more are suffering and dying because we can't get along.

Allah (swt) is calling us to unite and stay united for the long haul so we can stand strong.

Oh, hear the call, my brothers and sisters. **Worship Allah (swt) as Allah (swt) is worthy to be praised.**

Victory is ours; that is what we are taught and how we are raised.

The stories of the Prophets (as) are not for entertainment. **They are lessons from Allah (swt) passed down by the ancients.**

The stratagem that was used to slay Goliath. Muslims, **it is our turn** to use the same stratagem back at them to be triumphant: **faith, action, love!**

For it was love for their brothers that David and Goliath fought one on one, **but faith and action allowed David to be the one to overcome.**

Recommended Reading:

- Surah 9 At-Taubah Ayats 72-88
- Surah 33 Al-Ahzāb Ayats 9-27*
- Surah 4 An-Nisā Ayats 74-96
- Surah 2 Al-Baqarah Ayats 109-141 & 247-252**
- Surah 59 Al-Hashir Ayats 1-10

My Epitome 5

When I was about four years old, I could have died. It was only by the mercy of Allah (swt) that I did not. I fell out the second-floor window of a house. I had a near-death experience. Whether it was an actual vision or a dream, only Allah (swt) knows. I really can't say when I first had this vision; I only know that I saw it and that I was there. I was in the most angelic place. The walls were made of gold and glass, and the acoustics were so clear. It made my voice sound like music. I didn't want to leave, but someone was calling me, so I had to go. This vision has been with me for a very long time. I often wonder if that is what made me susceptible to religion. I have been seeking Allah (swt) all my life. I was in and out of churches, Catholic, Jehovah's Witnesses, Baptist, and Seventh Day Adventist.

Learning Christianity, of course, I learned about Paradise and Hell. Hell was scary, and Paradise seemed hard to obtain. So, I thought what I didn't know couldn't be held against me, WRONG!

Allah (swt) says in the Qur'an, Surah 38, Ayat 65, *"This day, we shall seal up their mouths, and their hands will speak to us, and their legs will bear witness to what they used to earn."*

So, we can lie to ourselves, but we can't lie to Allah

(swt). Anyway, that is what I thought at that time. So, I stopped going to church. However, I eventually started going back to church because I needed the Word. Life had taken such a toll on me, which made me seek Allah (swt) with a sincere heart. I sincerely read the Bible and the Qur'an several times.

I searched other religions as well, but because of their practices, they were not for me. I was convinced Islam was the religion for me because all religious books mention one God, but Islam has no association or partnership with the Creator. Nevertheless, I submitted and committed myself to Islam because Paradise is my goal. If Paradise is anything like my childhood vision, I want to go back there.

We all know death is a must. The reckoning is coming. Hell and Paradise are real, and our body parts will testify to what we know or don't know. We can lie to ourselves, but we cannot lie to Allah (swt).

Bism Allah Al-Rahman Al-Rahim

When You Know

Your heart, body, and soul will come together to acknowledge that **Allah (swt)** is the **One** and **Only God forever**, you know!

Although to the world, **you won't let it be known**. You heard Allah's calling to follow the path that leads you to His throne, you know!

Your eyes, hands, and feet will be your witness of that very moment. So, it is best to accept the calling instead of **making Allah (swt) your opponent,** you know!

Atheists and Evolutionists **hypothesize** about adaptive value and group cohesion. The effect of it on the brain, mind, and religion. Knowledge and acceptance of Allah (swt) as the **One and Only True God** was given to us **before we were even born**. Allah (swt) pulled our soul from Adam's loins, you know!

Perhaps you were not raised on the deen. Allah (swt) put signs in the earth and universe to remind us that he is **SUPREME**, you know!

When you know, **you know!** So does the Heavenly Host as they boast! Glorify Allah (swt) and give Him His praise because there will be **no excuses for how we were raised.**

Recommended Reading:

- Surah 7 Al-A'rāf Ayat 172-174**
- Surah 8 Al-Anfāl Ayats 13-14**
- Surah 2 Al-Baqarah Ayats 75-82**
- Surah 23 Al-Mu'minum Ayats 105-118*
- Surah 41 Ha Mim Al-Sajdah Ayats 19-24**
- Surah 59 Al-Hashir Ayats 22-24**
- Surah 58 Al-Mujadalah Ayats 5-7 & 20-22*
- Surah 47 Muhammad Ayats 29-34*
- Surah 30 Ar-Rūm Ayats 54-58**
- Surah 30 Ar-Rūm Ayats 54-58**

Bism Allah Al-Rahman Al-Rahim

My Soul

I see me **glistening** in a time not near, here or there. Yet, my presence is **everywhere!**

Echoing and bouncing from the crystal walls, my voice sounds like music because of the acoustics.

I exist, but I have no body. I move about **La De Da De**.

Yet, I hear someone calling me. My presence they demand to see!

The beauty and supreme peace I love it all, **but I must go** because **my Master has called.**

He says to me that it is your time to be born. **My mercy** I send with you to comfort the storms.

Now I am **embodying with this body.** My soul is restricted as to when I can move about **La De Da De.**

Yet, when I go to sleep, **my soul is free** to be wherever and whatever it chooses because my soul is free of me.

Wonders of a Treasure Trove to Allah

Allah (swt) has given us all a soul. Our souls **that are so magnificent our bodies cannot forever hold.**

The body will come to a final rest. **I pray** our souls have passed the test.

Recommended Reading:

- Surah 19 Maryam Ayats 8 & 60-67
- Surah 20 Ta'Ha Ayats 13-16
- Surah 7 Al-A'rāf Ayat 172
- Surah 89 Al-Farj Ayats 27-30
- Surah 43 Al-Zukhruf Ayats 67-73
- Surah 57 Al-Hadid Ayats 11-23

Bism Allah Al-Rahman Al-Rahim

I Want It

I want it. Oh Allah (swt), **I want Paradise**. I think about it all the time. **Please let me have that which is nice!**

On earth, I'm afraid of the jungle. So, I miss out on **all** its amazing wonders, **but** in Paradise, I get to graze in the grass with lions, tigers, and giraffes.

My own palace filled with gold, elevators, raised couches, rivers of milk and honey, **all of what is better than money.**

Eating my heart's desire, not concerned about the sun, shade, wind or fire. A mate to **satisfy my every desire and need.** I am begging you, Allah (swt), for Paradise, **I plead!**

I'm striving hard to live my life right. Please let me **achieve** my heart's delight.

Recommended Reading:

- Surah 55 Ar-Rahmah Ayats 46-78
- Surah 16 An-Nahl Ayats 31-32
- Surah 16 An-Nahl Ayats 110-111
- Surah 29 Al-Ankabūt Ayat 58
- Surah 76 Ad-Dahr Ayats 5-21
- Surah 56 Al-Wāqi'ah Ayats 13-40

Wonders of a Treasure Trove to Allah

- Surah 2 Al Baqarah Ayat 256
- Surah 89 Al-Farj Ayats 27-30
- Surah 43 Az-Zukruf Ayats 67-73

Bism Allah Al-Rahman Al-Rahim

It's Funny

It's funny. It seems I think more about **Hell** than I think of **Paradise**. I think I'm afraid of having things nice.

I always see the glass half empty instead of half full. I think that's because the world is so cruel.

I'm afraid of my behavior. I know my thoughts and actions don't always put me in Allah's favor.

Hell is surrounded by all the temptations in life: money, food, wine, and men. Sometimes, it seems it would be easier to give in.

Paradise, however, is surrounded by trials and tribulations enough to disturb your family's relations. It almost seems impossible to do. **This is why we need Allah (swt) to see us through.**

It's funny that I think about **Hell** more than **Paradise**, but if that's what works, I won't think about it twice.

Although I hope, as I practice my deen, Allah (swt) will bless me with faith to believe in my dream, **PARADISE!**

Wonders of a Treasure Trove to Allah

Recommended Reading:

- Surah 3 Al-Imran Ayat 195
- Surah 4 An-Nisā Ayats 124
- Sahih Al Bukhari Vol 8 Hadith 494
- Surah 43 Az-Zukhruf Ayats 67-73

Bism Allah Al-Rahman Al-Rahim

I Believe

I believe! **If I put Allah (swt) first** and follow His laws and commands, I could have the best of both worlds. Not material and wealth, but love, peace, and happiness, the things that truly allow the soul to rest.

Of course, the target is **Paradise**. For there, I am promised **everything** will be nice.

I believe! If I endure the trials and tribulations with gratefulness on earth, Allah (swt) will protect my family and me. But in heaven, I will be worry-free.

I believe! I can have **my cake and eat it, too,** because I believe the Qur'an to be true.

I believe! The earth is beautiful: the colors in the rainbow, which is Allah's promise; the flowers when they bloom, which is Allah's grace; the trees in the fall, which is Allah's sign. But I think the grass is greener on the other side. For in heaven, I will be able to graze with a lion and his pride.

I believe! **Sacrificing some of my desires** in this world is **purifying my soul.** Because when I get to heaven, I'm going to be adorned with bracelets of pearls and gold.

Wonders of a Treasure Trove to Allah

I believe! In this world, Allah (swt) subjected all creatures to mankind. But in heaven, men, jinn, angels, and all created beings will be **on one accord to praise Allah (swt),** which is the **GREATEST REWARD.**

I believe! If I could **stand** the test of time that Allah (swt) ordained, **patience** in this world would have been worth the wait. For Allah (swt) willing, I will enter Heaven's gates.

I believe! **If I put Allah (swt) first** and follow His laws and commands, life in this world would get easier day by day. And then, there is Paradise; wouldn't that be **NICE**?

Recommended Reading:

- Surah 3 Al-Imran Ayat 148
- Surah 41 Fussilat Ayats 31-33
- Surah 35 Fātir Ayats 33-35
- Surah 16 An-Nahl Ayats 30, 41 & 97
- Surah 43 Az-Zukhruf Ayats 67-73
- Surah 89 Al-Fajr Ayats 27-30

My Epitome 6

Matters of the heart are difficult. Relationships are difficult: mother/daughter, father/son, husband/wife, sister/sister, brother/brother, cousin/cousin, etc. They are all difficult. Whether you are living for Allah (swt) or not, relationships are difficult if you are not equally yoked. Parent/child relationships will never be equally yoked because of the age differences and because of the authority and honor bestowed upon parents. So, raising children can be difficult – not always, but in most cases, there is some tension, especially during the teenage years. Marriage is difficult, and relationships are difficult.

I myself wonder about the time when Allah (swt) banished Adam, Huwa, and Shaytan to earth, enemies to one another. How has that affected mankind's relationships with one another? Adam and Huwa were to be enemies to Shaytan and vice versa, but were husband and wife to be enemies to one another, also? For I sometimes feel I am sleeping with the enemy, an unseen enemy after my soul. Marriage is difficult. Relationships are difficult. I have given my all, at least, I think. I have overlooked faults. I changed my thinking and ways within the bounds of Allah's (swt) law in hopes of peace in my relationships, but peace is so far in between war.

If one person is trying to live right for Allah (swt) and if the other person is not, the person trying to live right for Allah (swt) is labeled judgmental, good doer, etc., and the person who is not living right is labeled wicked, a heathen, etc. If you are not equally yoked, your marriage is going to be difficult because of issues on how to raise the children, spend the finances, and even how to worship Allah (swt) when the Qur'an and Sunnah guide us. Marriage is difficult. Relationships are difficult. Unfortunately, most marriages will never be equally yoked because there are so many realms to consider, and it depends on what realm is most important to you. Is spirituality more important or education, financial status, appearance, etc.?

Again, I wonder if the hostility and chaos in marriage and relationships are, by design, designed so that we aren't in heavenly bliss here on earth because we are so in love with our mates/children/kin that we are willing to forsake our deen for their love. Hell is surrounded by humans' strongest desires. I am just saying.

Anyway, most of us will never be equally yoked. However, Allah (swt) is in the midst to comfort, guide, sway, and lead. Yes, Allah (swt) is the equalizer, the balance we seek in our marriages and relationships. So, if we have mates who are severely wicked or a little wicked, that is okay because righteous people can have bad habits. We should pray for ourselves first and foremost because wicked begets wicked, and bad behavior begets bad behavior. If you curse me, I curse you. If you hit me, I hit you, and so on. The most righteous person may not mean to react to bad behavior, but sometimes it is done instinctively, and sometimes it is just out of anger. So, we should pray for self first, then pray for our mates, our marriages, and our souls. However, we should never give our souls to the wicked. For wicked creeps, slowly blackening the heart because of verbal and physical abuse and neglect that leads to a lonely heart, which all could lead to anger, lies, infidelity, or divorce. Sleeping with the enemy, you can't live with them, and you can't live without them. At least, that is what Shaytan whispers. From the garden of bliss, Shaytan's goal has been to separate husband from wife. However, Allah (swt), in His merciful wisdom, blessed us with mercy, forgiveness, and love that we must impart in our marriages and our relationships. Allah (swt) knows what could have happened, what will happen, and what has already happened. Allah (swt) is All-Knowing.

It is not hard to forgive, but it is hard to forget if a person continues to do the same bad behavior over and over and over again: a drunkard continues to drink and abuse, an adulterous continues to cheat and hurt, a liar continues to manipulate and confuse, etc. Divorce is permissible in Islam but as a last resort. However, if your goal is to please Allah (swt) and your mate continues to bring out the wicked in you because of their bad behavior, run, GET OUT! Love should not cost us our deen. However, if we use the guidelines Allah (swt) set in the Qur'an and Sunnah in pursuing a mate before we get married, there is less chance of divorce, always keeping Allah (swt) in the midst.

Bism Allah Al-Rahman Al-Rahim

My Love

Oh Allah (swt), please bless me with **my beloved**. The **one** I keep dreaming of.

He is handsome, strong, and wise. **He listens** and reveres me as his lovely prize. **Most important,** he is on the deen. **He worships you, Allah (swt),** the one and only God, the Supreme!

He's family-oriented and financially set. **My wali approves** because him he has already vet.

He's loving, passionate, and **forgiving too**. Some may think he is too good to be true.

He is the one I keep dreaming of. **Please, Allah (swt), bless me with my beloved!**

Recommended Reading:

- Surah 30 Ar-Rūm Ayat 21
- Surah 28 Al-Qasas Ayat 56
- Surah 3 Al-Imran Ayats 103-104
- Surah 2 Al-Baqarah Ayats 186-187
- Surah 21 Al-Anbiyā' Ayats 89-90
- Surah 4 An-Nisā Ayats 66-70

Bism Allah Al-Rahman Al-Rahim
Open to Me

Open your heart to me, my love! We are married; our hearts and thoughts should not be so contrary.

You put **all before me**, and when you are near, **you are still so far**. It hurts my heart and **blackens it** with scars,

I desire to fulfill, **as your wife**, my worship of Allah (swt). **I must answer my Master's call.**

So, as your wife, I have humbled myself **in service to you**. Yet, you don't even notice **half** of what I do.

I usually wind up **swallowing my pride**. In hopes of rekindling **the love you had for me as your bride.**

Open your heart to me, my love! Show me some movement, a nudge, or a shove.

Truly if we part, **to us both,** it would be a loss and a heavy cost.

I know this because I have given you all of me. **With this plea, I'm praying that you'll see.**

Allah (swt) knows my heart. **Now**, it is time for you to do your part. **Open your heart to me, my love!**

Recommended Reading:

- Surah 3 Al-Iran Ayat 159
- Surah 40 Al-Mu'min Ayats 38-44
- Surah 30 Ar-Rūm Ayats 19-23
- Surah 33 Al-Ahzāb Ayats 70-7
- Surah 58 Al-Mujadalah Ayats 1-4

Bism Al-Rahman Al-Rahim
Woman

Woman, love me, know me, **give me** the benefit of the doubt. Don't be so ready to shout.

Communicating is sometimes hard for men to do. But we fear, we stress, **and sometimes life** is overwhelming, **and we need** a second breath.

When we come home from a hard day's work, **we want** to see a smile, a clean house, smell food cooking, and **not you looking irked.**

We all have our part to do to make a happy home. Don't put extra pressure on us **by trying to keep up with the Jones.**

Allah (swt) has blessed me with love for you, my wife. My plan is to **adore** you with contentment, passion, and a life without strife.

Recommended Reading:

- Surah 30 Ar-Rūm Ayats 19-23
- Surah 9 At-Taubah Ayats 7
- Surah 7 Al-A'rāf Ayat 189
- Surah 25 Furqan ayats 63-76

*Bism Allah Al-Rahman Al-Rahim*s

If Loving You

If loving you **was easy,** I wouldn't have to look for other things to be pleasing.

I fill my days with domestics and kin. **When really, I just want you as my friend.**

Definitely, **the nights are lonelier** than the days because **you'd rather watch** basketball or football plays.

Your faults, I do my best to overlook. **But my deen is constantly being shook.**

I am worn out from everybody, everything, and every game coming before me. I just want to be free.

I've stayed **thirteen years** because I wanted to give it my every try. **But I've got to stop** this weeping and this cry.

When I pray to Allah (swt) for an answer to my prayers, **my innermost thought** is, *why should I give him another year?*

If loving you **could have been easy**, we could have had a good life **because Allah (swt) knows I vowed to be a good wife.**

Wonders of a Treasure Trove to Allah

Recommended Reading:

- Surah 3 Al-Imran Ayat 159
- Surah 40 Al-Mu'min Ayats 38-44
- Surah 33 Al-Ahzāb Ayats 35-36 & 49
- Surah 2 Al-Baqarah Ayats 35-39
- Surah 9 At-Taubah Ayats 70-71
- Surah 24 An-Nūr Ayats 26-35

Bism Allah Al-Rahman Al-Rahim

To You I Tweet

Like the blackbird, you lured my heart with song. Your words, your swag, your voice, I thought you could do no wrong.

Time has passed, and the true you has emerged. Your words no longer give me that loving urge.

Allah (swt) comes first and foremost to me. That hold you had: Allah (swt) has set me free.

So, to you, love, I tweet with my heart I pour. **You touched me deeply**. Gee, you sure did score.

Like times we have met and spoke not a tweet because you often denied me of touching you sweet.

I've always tried loving you with lots of passion, but you **wouldn't** allow me to relax in my own fashion.

So, to you, I tweet, love, with my heart I pour. **Unlike the blackbird**, now that I don't love, I find you a bore so you can soar.

Recommended Reading:

- Surah 33 Al-Ahzāb Ayats 35-36 & 49

Wonders of a Treasure Trove to Allah

- Surah 2 Al-Baqarah Ayats 223-242
- Surah 37 As-Saffāt Ayats 22-62
- Surah 30 Ar-Rūm Ayats 17-30

Bism Allah Al-Rahman Al-Rahim
Do You Really Listen

You say I don't talk, **but do you really listen?** **I am not** trying to please your family and friends to fit in.

I know family is a package deal, but they don't get to decide **how I provide our meals.**

You always talk about how **you want me out of the streets,** but when you can't get the **Louis Vuitton, you squeak, squeak, squeak!**

Allah (swt) has opened my eyes to what is right. **I am done with the streets.** Halal work is what I seek.

You married a man **who is now** on his deen. I am far from perfect, but as long as I try, I believe our marriage is worth it.

So, stop! Please stop giving me mixed messages about how to please you because it is to Allah (swt) that I want us to be true.

So, no, you can't get that Louis Vuitton **if I must make money doing stuff that is haram.**

I don't care how your family and friends are living. I am grateful and appreciative of what Allah (swt) has given.

Recommended Reading:

- Surah 30 Ar-Rūm Ayats 17-27
- Surah 7 Al-A'rāf 189
- Surah 25 Furqān Ayats 63-76

Bism Allah Al-Rahman Al-Rahim
A Vicious Cycle

You say it is me. **I say it is you.** We keep disputing about the same things no matter what we do.

You hurt me, and I hurt you. **A vicious cycle** that goes round and round, and we are both walking around with all kinds of frowns.

Shaytan will continue to remind us of our pain. So, we are constantly faulting one another with blame.

Oh! Our issues are severe, and they are clear.

You say I am never satisfied, and I say you never spend quality time. All the while, Shaytan is playing with our minds.

So, join me in prayer. **Let us show Allah (swt) it is the loss of His love that we fear.**

And **if** it be Allah's will, our lives **will change for the better** because we have changed to practice our deen to the letter.

Recommended Reading:

- Surah 30 Ar-Rūm Ayats 17-27

Wonders of a Treasure Trove to Allah

- Surah 7 Al-A'rāf 189
- Surah 39 Az-Zumar Ayats 9-18
- Surah 25 Furqān 63-76
- Surah 58 Al-Mujadalah Ayats 1-4

Bism Allah Al-Rahman Al-Rahim

Happiness

Happiness, where are you? **I miss you terribly!** Please come back because I miss you and that is a fact.

You bring me joy, and you make me smile. To be in your presence, I would walk many miles.

Your visits are so few and far in between, but when you are around, your aura, **oh your aura,** makes me feel like a queen.

The sky is bluer. The air feels clean. My mood is happy, and I have no desire to be mean.

Happiness, where are you? I need you now because I am starting to feel sad, and for me, that can be really bad.

Creepy whisperers are telling me that you and I are through **and that I cannot** count on you to help me with these blues.

I know that is a lie, because although your visits are few and far in between, you have been a constant and on what I can lean.

Surely, after hardship comes ease; one hardship, two ease. **Allah (swt) knows how to please.**

Recommended Reading:
- Surah 109 Al-Kāfirūn Ayats 1-6
- Surah 10 Yūnus Ayats 104-109
- Surah 3 Al-Imran Ayat 148
- Surah 35 Fātir Ayats 29-35
- Surah 41 HaMim Al-sajdah Ayats 30-36
- Surah 16 An-Nahl Ayats 30-32

Epitome 7

When Allah (swt) decrees a thing, the benefits are usually enormous. Fasting has been prescribed for mankind. However, I speak now of the fast for the Muslims. We are to abstain from sex, eating, and drinking from sunup to sundown, which allows the body to restore its healing capabilities. We are to abstain from idle talk always, but especially during the month of fasting, which warns us to humble ourselves. We are to engage in much prayer and those who can prostrate benefit spiritually as well as physically because of the movement.

The benefits of fasting are enormous. However, what the body and soul consume can be detrimental to a person. Too much consumption of food can damage the body in so many ways, like diabetes, cancer, allergies, or death. As a child, my family could not afford what I thought was good food like Pizza Hut, McDonald's, Burger King, Red Lobster, etc. So, when and if we experienced that kind of outing, it was few and far in between and a treat, although I can't remember an outing like that because it was 13 of us: 11 children, my mom, and my stepdad.

However, when I got older and was able to treat myself, food became a vice along with other vices, but food was my favorite. I indulged in pizza, burgers, steaks, and seafood, etc. I wanted it all and as much as I could eat. So, when the market for All-You-Can-Eat restaurants became popular, I was a patron. All-You-Can-Eat restaurants, we thought so great, but in reality, the concept of All-You-Can-Eat restaurants is an insulin death trap. The body is like a trash compactor. It takes in food, grinds it up, and then eliminates the waste. However, if we overeat over and over again without giving the body a chance to eliminate the waste properly, it stores up in our organs as too much glucose, causing all kinds of health problems.

The concept of All-You-Can-Eat restaurants was never to benefit the consumer, nor did it benefit humanity because what they should have called it was All-You-Can-Waste. People pile their plates with a lot of food only to waste it, and all I can think of when I see that is all the starving people around the world. Not to mention the health hazard of all the hands touching the same utensils, people breathing over the food, kids playing with the food, etc. The All-You-Can-Eat concept eventually became unpopular with me. Eating out is risky in its own right. I try not to risk my health at All-You-Can-Eat restaurants if I can avoid them, especially since the COVID-19 pandemic. However, in some vacation spots, you can't avoid it.

Anyway, eating too much food, especially the wrong food, is detrimental to our health. The body needs time between meals to regulate the process to eliminate the waste properly. Fasting has been prescribed for mankind for a reason, and recently, scientists are really realizing the benefits of fasting for the body. Fasting allows the body to heal itself by letting the organs, like the kidneys and liver, balance the distribution of what goes to the blood. Of course, I am not a doctor or scientist so research digestion if you please. The point is what Allah (swt) decreed for mankind from Prophet Adam (as) to us is what scientists are just realizing.

Allah (swt) decreed that we should eat halal food, which means we should care how the animals are raised and slaughtered and that they are slaughtered in the name of Allah (swt). This is how the Qur'an reads. However, some people say you only need to pray over your food in the name of Allah (swt), not caring whether it was slaughtered in the name of Allah (swt). I say to you your worship and to me my worship. I am not a scholar.

However, what we put in our bodies must be scrutinized. The food manufacturers don't care about our health; they are about making a profit, and they advertise the most delicious-looking junk food we most desire. The junk that we put in our bodies is killing us. I have been overweight since my 40s and truly haven't taken my health seriously until now, in my 60s, and I am still struggling. I always knew that I should eat less and exercise more, but I was stuck, stuck in useless thinking, laziness, and depression, and food had been my only vice since I became Muslim. I pampered myself with food and, unfortunately, I still do sometimes.

The saving grace is that food can also be healing. Scientists are re-discovering the intricate ways to use fasting and food as a healing for the body – the methods our ancient ancestors used. We don't need three heavy meals a day. We need to allow time between meals for the body to naturally push the nutrients through the organs and blood and eliminate the waste.

Fasting was not only prescribed for the body; it was prescribed for the soul also. Just as the body must be nourished properly, so must the soul. Every day, as much as we can, we should refrain from backbiting, fornicating, lying, cheating, stealing, killing, etc. We should pray our five daily prayers and give Allah (swt) much praise. However, it is all obligatory that one does so in the month of Ramadan, and Allah (swt) has decreed it so we can replenish our souls to fight off the whispers of Shaytan.

Regina Woods

Bism Allah Al-Rahman Al-Rahim

Food

Food, yum! So delicious! Cakes, pies, and chocolate, trying to resist seems so ridiculous.

But our bodies are truly temples. **Allah (swt) created us all unique.** It is just that simple.

Healing is part of our **DNA.** As long as we don't block our cell's pathways.

Good food, bad food, is there really such a thing? Steak, potatoes, and my favorite, fried chicken wings.

Some foods are halal, and some foods are haram. Allah (swt) allowed it all to be explained in the Qur'an.

A three-course meal three times a day is way too much food, especially if we are consuming all the bad foods that we think are so good.

Food, yum! So delicious! We just have to respect our temples because Allah (swt) created us all unique. It is just that simple.

Recommended Reading:

- Surah 17 Al-Isrā' Ayats 81-84

Wonders of a Treasure Trove to Allah

- Surah 2 Al-Baqarah Ayats 168-176 & 61
- Surah 6 Al-An'ām Ayats 118-121
- Surah 56 Al-Wāqi'ah Ayats 10-24
- Surah 5 Al-Ma'idah Ayats 3-5

Bism Allah Al-Rahman Al-Rahim

Jump

Jump, run, skip, walk, **move that body!** We can't cleanse our bodies and souls if all we do is talk.

We should love ourselves, long legs, dark skin/light skin, and flaws, for none of us are perfect that is for sure by far.

Sweat is good for the body, mind, and soul. It rejuvenates us when we are feeling useless and old.

Feelings are mind over matter, but exercise prevents us from getting fatter.

For surely, beauty is only in the eye of the beholder but denying ourselves the best of us is like giving ourselves the cold shoulder.

Jump to it. Get that exercise to maximize your energy – the energy that allows us to ward off our enemy.

Fasting is prescribed to regenerate our minds, souls, and bodies in hopes of love and respect for ourselves and one another, but most important, love for our Creator and no other.

Recommended Reading:

- Surah 2 Al-Baqarah Ayats 183-187
- Surah 109 Al-Kāfirūn Ayats 1-6

Bism Allah Al-Rahman Al-Rahim
Talk About It

Talk about it. **Talk about the good things in life**, not what creates havoc and strife.

The way of the world today is to devour and destroy others' characters and then toss them away.

Eating the flesh of our brothers or sisters is just nasty, but that is what we will eat if we continue to speak of others crafty.

Words **penetrate** the soul because it is important for all of us to feel self-worth to be whole.

We should love for our brothers and sisters what we love for ourselves: **a God-conscious** health, and wealth.

Talk about it. **Talk about the good things in life,** not what creates havoc and strife.

Recommended Reading:
- Surah 26 An-Nūr Ayat 26*
- Surah 49 Al-Hujurāt Ayats 9-18
- Surah 39 Az-Zumar Ayats 33-39
- Surah 56 Al-Wāqi'ah Ayats 25-38
- Surah 104 Al-Humazah Ayats 1-9

Wonders of a Treasure Trove to Allah

Bism Allah Al-Rahman Al-Rahim
The Will

Allah (swt) gave us the will to choose whom and what we would worship. **Mankind bore it.** Unlike the heavens, earth, and mountains, they refused because they were afraid to commit.

The will to choose, in most cases, we lose.

Prophet Adam (as) was **given a wife and a garden** with all its delight. But one command to not touch the tree, that desire he could not fight.

The choices in life are many. Who shall we worship? Who shall we marry? How shall we obtain our wealth? In what region shall we live in?

The will to choose, in most cases, we lose.

Sometimes in our lives, **we must learn to pray thy will of the Lord be done** and sincerely mean it. For thy will of Allah (swt) is to whom we must submit.

Give the choice in every decision back to Allah (swt). **O Allah,** give me the perseverance, patience, and acceptance of **thy will** so I can live joyously in this world of strife.

Recommended Reading:
- Surah 39 Az-Zumar 9-18
- Surah 103 Al-Asr Ayats 1-3
- Surah 109 Al-Kāfirūn Ayats 1-6
- Surah 114 An-Nas Ayats 1-6

Bism Allah Al-Rahman Al-Rahim

Merciful

Merciful Lord, Gracious God, I thank you for your mercy. Your **99 names** you have given us to call upon you I know as a courtesy.

Forgiveness is granted to whomever sincerely repents regardless of what vile, scrupulous intent.

Merciful Lord, Gracious God, I thank you for your mercy. I pray my worship will prove me to be worthy.

Recommended Reading:
- Surah 53 An-Najm Ayats 31-64
- Surah 39 Az-Zumar Ayat 53-67
- Surah 26 Ash-Shu'rā Ayats 81-90
- Surah 25 Furqān Ayat 68
- Surah 7 Al-A'rāf Ayats 180-188
- Surah 109 Al-Kāfirūn Ayats 1-6
- Surah 59 Al-Hashir Ayats 20-24

Bism Allah Al-Rahman Al-Rahim
Spreading the Love

Spreading love, which is the word, is **hard to do** when people **turn their noses up at you.**

Eyes rolling, **lips** twisting just because **you asked them to pray.** Protection they're going to wish they had throughout their day.

Shaytan has nearly put this world on lockdown. Men, women, and children talking, looking, and acting like clowns.

Men dressing like women, women dressing like men, the product of such actions **makes your head spin.**

Love, you think would be easy, **but it is not.** Because to truly love, you bite your tongue, must have patience, **and ignore people's faults a lot.**

Spreading love, which is the word, is hard to do. I know this must be my test because Paradise is where I want to rest.

Hell is surrounded by all one's delights, but Paradise is surrounded by trials and tribulations, so **for love,** I must be patient.

Patience is faith, steadfastness, and action, too. We must do what we can to spread the love which is Allah's

Wonders of a Treasure Trove to Allah

word. Allah's kingdom is the Ultimate, the Glorious, and if achieved, we will be victorious.

Recommended Reading:
- Surah 2 Al-Baqarah Ayat 45 & 155-157*
- Surah 10 Yūnus Ayats 15-18 & 40-44*
- Surah 103 Al-Asr Ayats 1-3**
- Surah 87 Al-Alā Ayats 1-19
- Surah 84 Al-Inshiqāq Ayats 1-25*
- Surah 77 Al-Mursalāt Ayats 1-13***
- Surah 22 Al-Hajj Ayats 72-78**
- Surah 41 Ha mim Al Sajdah Ayats 33-36
- Surah 47 Muhammad Ayats 19-38**
- Surah 64 Al-Taghabun Ayats 14-18**
- Surah 51 Az-Zāryiāt Ayats 47-60*
- Hadith Sahih Muslim 2823**

Bism Allah Al-Rahman Al-Rahim

I'm Stuck Like That

Oh Allah! Did you **See** that?

I saved my best friend, and she didn't have my back, but I keep doing it again and again.

Oh Allah! Did you **Hear** that?

My husband promised he would stop putting everything and everyone before me, but I am still last on his list even though I have plead.

Oh Allah! Did you **Taste** that?

I am savoring the sweet taste of victory because I relinquished the control people had over me. Now, I am on my lifelong quest. Islam is the religion I have rest.

Oh Allah! Did you **Smell** that?

I smell the scent of freedom in the air because you taught me to really care. It doesn't matter what people do or don't do as long as you don't let them change the good in you.

Oh Allah! Did you **Feel** that?

Wonders of a Treasure Trove to Allah

Your words give me such a chill because I find Islam to be the *Reeal Deeal*. So now my life is new. I am looking to recruit a whole new crew.

I know some of you think there are only five senses from Allah (swt), but these senses right here are the **GREATEST OF THEM ALL!**

Oh Allah! Did you **Think** that?

A thought, a dream, a vision, and a memory, too, are all gifts from Allah (swt) to you. So, use these senses to unlock life mysteries and clues because, in the world, there are all kinds of signs for you. **Now I'm on my life journey to chat because I am stuck like that.**

Recommended Reading:
- Surah 7 Al-A'rāf Ayats 195-201
- Surah 17 Al-Isrā Ayats 36-38
- Surah 16 An-Nahl Ayats 77-79 & 125-128
- Surah 38 Sād Ayats 45-51*
- Surah 109 Al-Kāfirūn Ayats 1-6
- Surah 72 Al-Jinn Ayats 19-28
- Surah 42 Ash-Shū-ura Ayats 15-16
- Surah 23 Al-Mu'minūn Ayat 78

Abu Hurairah (may Allah be pleased with him) narrated that the Messenger of Allah (saw) said: *"Allah, the Most High said: 'I am as My slave thinks of Me, and I am with him when he remembers Me. If he remembers Me to himself, I remember him to Myself, and if he remembers Me in a gathering, I remember him in a gathering better than that. And if he seeks to draw nearer to Me by a hand span, I draw nearer to him by a forearm's length, and if he comes to Me by a forearm's length, I draw near to him by an arm's length. And if he comes to Me walking, I come to him quickly.'"*

Grade: Sahih (Darussalam)

Reference: Jami' at-Tirmidhi 3603

In-book reference: Book 48, Hadith 234

English translation.: Vol. 6, Book 46, Hadith 3603

Index

Charles Darwin (12 February 1809-19 April 1882) was a British naturalist who proposed the theory of biological evolution by natural selection (1859 Origin of Species).

Darwin defined evolution as "descent with modification," the idea that species change over time, give rise to a new species, and share a common ancestor.

Species are defined as similar organisms that can interbreed and produce healthy, fertile offspring.

Natural selection, because resources are limited in nature, organisms with heritable traits that favor survival and reproduction will tend to leave more offspring than their peers, causing the trait to increase in frequency over generations.

Natural selection causes populations to become adapted, or increasingly well-suited, to their environment over time. Natural selection depends on the environment and requires existing heritable variation in a group.

While Charles Darwin's theory of evolution has been a great contribution to science because the environment does have its role in the development and adaptation of many species, its speculation about mankind's creation is invalid. Molecular biology in the 20th and 21st centuries has given proof that apes, with their 48 chromosomes, are not compatible with mankind with their 46 chromosomes. Scientists try to explain this major karyotypic difference, which they claimed was caused by the fusion of two ancestral chromosomes to form human chromosomes and subsequent inactivation of one of the two original centromeres. In other words, the man-ape went extinct, which they are still guessing about.

Molecular biology, by utilizing modern methods of investigation, such as X-ray diffraction and electron microscopy, to explore levels of cellular organization beyond that visible with a light microscope – the ultrastructure of the cell – new concepts of cellular function were produced. As a result, the study of the molecular organization of the cell has had a tremendous impact on biology and has led directly to the convergence of many different scientific disciplines to acquire a better understanding of life processes. Technologies such as DNA sequencing and polymerase chain reaction also were developed, allowing biologists to peer into the genetic blueprints that give rise to organisms.

The first-generation sequencing technologies emerged in the 1970s and were followed several decades later by so-called next-generation sequencing technologies, which were superior in speed and cost-efficiency. Next generation sequencing provided researchers with massive amounts of genetic data, typically gigabases in size (1 gigabase =1,000,000,000 base pairs of DNA). Bioinformatics, which linked biological data with tools and techniques for <u>data analysis</u>, storage, and distribution, became an increasingly important part of biological studies, particularly those involving very large sets of genetic data.

Genetic engineering enabled researchers to recombine nuclei acids and thereby modify organisms' genetic codes, giving the organisms new abilities or eliminating undesirable traits. Those developments were followed by advances in <u>cloning</u> technologies, which led to the generation in 1996 of Dolly, the sheep, the first clone of an adult mammal. Together, recombinant DNA technology and reproductive cloning (the method used to produce a living animal clone) facilitated great progress in the development of <u>genetically modified organisms</u> (GMOs). Such organisms became crucial components of biomedical research, where genetically modified (GM) mice and other animals were developed to model certain human diseases, thereby facilitating the investigation of new therapies and factors that cause disease. What was researched and designed for medicine became a fashion for designer babies and animal crossbreeding, and only Allah (swt) knows what other kinds of experiments scientists are doing.

Lion and Tiger Hybridization is the process in which both lion and tiger are successfully crossbred to produce offspring. Such offspring are called hybrid offspring. Furthermore, within such hybridization, if the male is a lion and the female is a tiger (tigress), then the hybrid offspring is termed a liger. Vice versa, if the male is a tiger and the female is a lion (lioness), then the hybrid offspring is called a tigon.

Human impact on the environment has resulted in an increase in the interbreeding between regional species, and the proliferation of introduced species worldwide has also resulted in the increase in hybridization.

The Kunga, the donkey-like creature, is considered to be the oldest hybrid bred by humans. The kungas of Syro-Mesopotamia were ancient equines that roamed the region 4,500 years ago. Arriving long before domesticated horses did, the stocky horse-like animals were highly valued and used for pulling four-wheeled wagons into battle, reports James Gorman for the New York Times.

A genetic analysis using ancient skeletal remains, genetic material from the last surviving Syrian wild ass, and an investigation of the evolutionary history of the genus Equus revealed that the kunga was the cross of a female donkey (Equus Africanus asinus) and a male Syrian wild ass (Equus Hemionus Hemippus), reports Isaac Schultz for

Wonders of a Treasure Trove to Allah

Gizmodo. Harsh desert conditions poorly preserved DNA from the 25 skeletons obtained from the Umm eel-Marra site, so researchers use advanced sequencing methods to compare the bits and pieces of DNA, Science reports. Researchers then compared the results to an 11,000-year-old equid sample taken from the Gobekli Tepe archaeological site in Turkey and genetic material taken from a preserved museum specimen of the last surviving wild Syrian ass that went extinct in 1929 per Gismodo. Using Y-chromosome fragments, the team found that the kunga's paternal lineage belonged to the Syrian wild ass and matched the species of the sample from Turkey. They also confirmed donkeys were the maternal lineage, Gizmodo reports. Like other hybrids in the animal kingdom, such as the mule or the liger, the kunga were sterile. They had to be intentionally bred by mating a female donkey with a male wild ass, per Gizmodo.

That being said, if true, mankind has been experimenting with changing the nature of what Allah (swt) created for a very long time, and only Allah (swt) knows the true effect of what has been done, what is being done, and what is going to be done on plants, animal, the earth and mankind.

Sir Isaac Newton (25 December 1642-20 March 1726) was an English polymath active as a mathematician, physicist, astronomer, alchemist, theologian, and author who was described in his time as a natural philosopher. Newton also made seminal contributions to optics and shared credit with German mathematician Gottfried Wilhelm Leibriz. In Newton's book *Philosophies Naturalis Principia Mathematica*, he formulated the laws of motion and universal gravitation that formed the dominant scientific viewpoint for centuries until it was superseded by the theory of relativity (Albert Einstein 14 March 1879-18 April 1955, the equation $E=mc^2$).

Newton used his mathematical description of gravity to derive Kepler's laws of planetary motion, account for tides, the trajectories of comets, the precession of the equinoxes, and other phenomena, eradicating doubt about the Solar System's heliocentricity. He demonstrated that the motion of objects on Earth and celestial bodies could be accounted for by the same principles.

www.ingramcontent.com/pod-product-compliance
Lightning Source LLC
LaVergne TN
LVHW021952060526
838201LV00049B/1672